P9-BHV-172

PICKING UP THE PIECES

PICKING UP THE PIECES
HEALING OURSELVES AFTER PERSONAL LOSS

Barbara Hansen, Ph.D.

Taylor Publishing Company
Dallas, Texas

Designed by Deborah Jackson-Jones

Copyright © 1990 by Barbara Hansen

All rights reserved.

No part of this book may be reproduced in any form
without written permission from the publisher.

Published by Taylor Publishing Company
                1550 West Mockingbird Lane
                Dallas, Texas 75235

Library of Congress Cataloging-in-Publication Data
Hansen, Barbara, 1935-
      Picking up the pieces : healing ourselves after
personal loss /
    Barbara Hansen.
          p.   cm.
      ISBN 0-87833-763-6 : $14.95
      1. Loss (Psychology)   2. Hansen, Barbara, 1935–
    3. Paraplegics—United States—Psychology.   4. Loss
(Psychology)-
    -Case studies.   I. Title.
    BF575.D34H35   1990
    155.9'3—dc20   90-35323
                                                    CIP

Printed in the United States of America

10 9 8 7 6 5 4 3 2 1

To my parents, Ruth and Joe,
and
my friend Rebecca Maureen,
all of whom made my mending possible

CONTENTS

PREFACE

Did life just deal you a lousy hand?

Maybe your husband decided he didn't want to be a part of your life anymore, and you're working your way through an unwanted divorce. Or your mother just died, leaving you without the best friend you ever had. Or your son was in a car wreck and now must live the remainder of his life in a wheelchair. Or the managerial position for which you worked thirty years was just given to a younger man. Or the by-pass surgery which saved your life left you with more limitations than you bargained for.

I've written this book for everyone who has experienced a loss so great that life seems meaningless. If you're one of these people, right now you aren't sure that living makes much sense. Staring at the ceiling in the middle of the night, you wonder if suicide might be preferable to the eternal emptiness that is masquerading as your life. You feel like a leaf in the wind blown about by the forces of fate, and fate hasn't been kind.

If this sounds familiar, you may want to read this book. It was written for people like you.

In it I discuss various avenues which can bring meaning back into your life. As a result of being a paraplegic for over thirty years, I've experienced every aspect of grief.

When I was nineteen, my spinal cord was severed in an automobile accident. Picking up the pieces of my shattered life, I started on a life-long search for wholeness. While doing so, I met many other fragmented people making the same search. As an English professor, I heard the frustration and despair of students dealing with loss; as a public speaker, I listened to my audiences express similar feelings of hopelessness. Seldom did a week go by that I didn't hear someone telling me about a loss that ripped his life to shreds.

As I listened, it became clear that society measures success differently than I do. Since being paralyzed I've earned B.S., M.A., and Ph.D. degrees in English, taught twenty-eight years in two state universities, counseled numerous students going through loss, climbed from instructor to associate professor, won honors and fellowships, bought my own home, and acquired financial security. So, in society's eyes I'm a success.

Yet, success isn't something we acquire at the end of a journey; rather, it's how we respond to the journey itself. Success doesn't come from money, prestige, or degrees; it's a process, not a product. It's not where we are or what we've got; it's how we felt about ourselves and others as we were getting there.

Success comes from finding meaning in life—in spite of loss.

This meaning doesn't just happen by chance. We've all seen the same kind of loss devastate one person while making another stronger. "Why?" we ask. "Why do some people successfully heal while others stay shattered?"

Although many people believe they are the victims of circumstance and have no control over their destiny, I've found that circumstances—in and of themselves—are not as significant as a person's attitude toward them and the internal resources she has cultivated to deal with them.

Response to loss is a very individual matter. Each step back to wholeness is a solitary, private step, and no one can take those steps for you. This book can't heal your broken life. You, and you alone, can do that. It can, however, help you find the strength to pick up the pieces of that life and create wholeness again. Since no one can tell someone else how to heal, I haven't tried. What I've written is not magical, miraculous, nor mandatory. It's simply a record of what I have discovered in grieving my own loss and in being beside others grieving theirs.

I want to thank all my students and former students who have shared their lives and losses with me. Knowing them has hastened my own healing. Although the substance and details of the case histories in the book are authentic, names and identities have been changed to protect the confidentiality of friendship.

I especially want to thank my friend Rebecca McDaniel for her early support and unfailing encouragement. Although I'd kept notes for years as insurance against the day I'd "tell the world what I've learned," it was Rebecca's belief in me that nudged my nebulous dream into reality. As a result, fragments of ideas which had been stored in journals and on notecards finally took shape and became a manuscript. She has been involved in this book from inception to completion, reading and discussing with me each chapter as it was written and editing every revision that followed.

While lying in the hospital after the wreck, I had plenty of time to think. As I filed through my bank of accumulated knowledge, a statement by Albert Schweitzer kept going through my mind: "Anyone who has had pain is obligated to help someone going through pain."

That's what this book is all about.

LIFE DEALS
EVERYONE SOME
LOUSY HANDS

*"Life's a tumble-about thing
of ups and downs."*
Benjamin Disraeli, *Sybil*

Looking at the twenty-eight-year-old woman sitting in the office, I watched as she unsuccessfully tried to control the tears streaming down her face. Reaching for the tissues I keep for such occasions, I waited as she desperately tried to gain her composure.

"I really don't want to bother you," she sobbed, "but I'm so lonely I could die." Then a small half-smile crossed her tear-stained face as she added, "That's a hyperbole, isn't it?" As her English professor I'd

3

taught her the literary term the previous year. Now as her friend and former teacher, I assured her that it was, indeed, hyperbole and quickly added, "But that's not the point. At this moment you're so lonely that you'd like to die, and that's not exaggeration. That's just a fact."

WHY DO I STILL HURT SO MUCH?

Knowing she had been divorced less than a year, I listened as she explained the incident which had brought her into my office. "I saw Mark at the grocery last night, and it was terrible. I mean—it was just nothing. Just surface nothing," she said. "After not seeing each other for weeks, we meet unexpectedly in the soft drink aisle of Krogers, and he treats me like any other nobody buying diet Pepsi! Good Lord, I was his wife! We have two children! Why doesn't he miss me like I miss him? Why doesn't he want me like I want him? I'm so tired of being lonely and rejected. I'm sick of life. I want him so badly that I hurt all over. I ache to be wanted, and what happens? We see each other, and absolutely nothing happens. Why can't I get over this? It's been a year now. Why do I still hurt so much?"

She and I both knew that I didn't have the answers to any of her questions, but we also knew that she needed to ask them. As I listened, she poured out her

4

feelings of frustration and loneliness. As she talked, she became calmer. About an hour later she was emotionally drained, but dry-eyed. As she picked up her purse and books, smoothed her hair, and turned to leave, she said, "No one but you understands what I'm going through."

WHY IS MY LIFE SO HOPELESS?

Later that same week my home phone rang just as I was getting ready for bed. On the other end of the line was a voice I had grown to know well. It belonged to one of my former students who had experienced too many losses in too short a time. Death, drugs, and divorce had all played havoc with her life. It was not unusual for her to reach out when a new crisis occurred.

"I want to escape again. Life is closing in and trapping me," she said, trying to mask the hysteria in her voice. "I feel it's hopeless."

Knowing she had attempted suicide twice before and realizing it was not the time for non-directive listening, I plunged into the problem at hand. As I had expected, another loss had entered her life. The man she had been sharing her life and apartment with for the last six months had decided to go his own way, leaving her facing yet another rejection.

No, It Isn't Fair

"Life isn't fair," she sobbed. "No," I agreed. "Life isn't fair. But it never has been. Why is it worse right now?"

"Nathan left me. Why does everyone leave me? I will never, absolutely never, become attached to another person. It's just not worth the pain."

She continued, "When my brother was killed in a car crash, my whole life fell apart. Losing him was terrible, but Mother and I became really close after that, almost like sisters. Just when I was beginning to think that life made some sense, Mother decided to remarry. After the marriage, she no longer needed me. I mean, she had a new husband, and I just wasn't important like I had been."

I listened, remembering how the literal loss of her brother and the perceived loss of her mother had plunged her into a series of sexual affairs, each of which had failed to bring the security she was seeking. Nathan, her most recent partner, had been the replacement for Carl, a man who had skillfully managed to make her totally dependent on him, and on drugs, before dropping her for another girl.

"It just isn't fair," she continued. "Nathan's been gone two days now, and I just know he's not coming back. Look at me! Every single time I let myself love someone, I get hurt." Her words came tumbling on

6

top of each other as she tried unsuccessfully to verbalize her despair.

Sensing that she was growing calmer, I took a gamble and asked, "What's your worst fear right now?" I knew I'd hit the right nerve when she quickly replied, "That I'll try to kill myself. Every day it's an effort to live. I can't connect with life anymore. I'm not close to anyone. When Nathan seemed to need me, I tried, really tried, to forget all Carl's dirty tricks. But it was all for nothing. Even if Nathan came back tomorrow, I know that I wouldn't be able to trust him. In fact, I'm afraid to trust anyone. I feel so isolated. Why do I get all the bad breaks?"

Her talking and my listening went on for over an hour until she assured me that she "felt better." Before she hung up, I heard an echo from a few days earlier, "No one but you knows what I'm going through. You're the only one who understands."

REJECTION AND LOSS ARE UNIVERSAL

That, of course, was not true. There were many people who could, and would, have understood what both women were going through. When loss in any form enters our lives, we all have similar reactions.

◆ We all feel totally alone and misunderstood.

7

◆ We feel as if our life is breaking into fragments.

◆ We learn that loss breaks more than just our hearts; it breaks our souls.

◆ We feel broken beyond repair.

This process of breaking is a painful, but normal, part of any loss.

Are You Hurting?

Fill in the blank with 3, 2, or 1, using the following scale:

   (3) Very true   (2) Somewhat true   (1) Not true

_____ 1. Each day is a 24-hour ordeal to be gotten through by hiding my despair and putting on a happy face for the public.

_____ 2. I dread going to bed at night, knowing the next hours will be filled with sleeplessness and staring at the ceiling.

_____ 3. In the morning when halfway between sleep and wakefulness, I have the vague sensation that something is terribly wrong.

_____ 4. After the alarm rings, I wish I could stay in the house all day, avoiding all contact with people and life.

_____ 5. Listening to the lyrics of many songs is painful, making me cry uncontrollably as they awaken painful emotions.

—— 6. I constantly eat everything I can get my hands on, even when I'm not hungry. (or) Food has lost all appeal; I have to force myself to eat.

—— 7. My use of alcohol (or) cigarettes (or) coffee has gone from moderate to constant.

—— 8. I feel as if I'm a victim who doesn't deserve the rotten circumstances that life has handed me.

—— 9. I want to skip the holidays this year. They only intensify my anguish as I go through the motions of traditions, feeling like an outsider.

—— 10. Life seems senseless and useless. At times dying seems preferable to the life I am now leading.

If your score is 15 or higher, chances are great that loss has broken your life.

WHY ISN'T THERE ANYONE WHO UNDERSTANDS ME?

On an intellectual level we know that thousands of people have experienced losses similar to ours, but our emotional level keeps telling us that no one in the world has ever felt as totally rejected and cheated as we do. No one, we're sure, could possibly have felt the same tearing pain and agony which haunts us constantly. No one could ever have experienced the emptiness, the loneliness, which fills every waking minute and then has the nerve to creep into our dreams at night. No one really understands what we're going through.

But we wish desperately that someone did.

Students, and former students, often discover that I'm that someone. Each September as the days grow crisp and the trees turn magnificent shades of gold and amber, I return to my job as teacher at a large Midwestern university. Each year on the first day of fall quarter, I make four entries into the classroom. Four classes of eager, apprehensive students try desperately to stifle their surprise as they discover that their English professor didn't walk in; she and her Everest and Jennings wheelchair rolled in together. Not a word needs to be spoken. From that first day on, the students know that loss has been an integral part of my life. So it's only natural that in the months, years, and yes, even decades to follow, some of these students will turn to me when going through their own private loss.

For many years I assumed that nothing but chance coincidence brought the steady steam of students to my office and my home. "I just happen to be the right person at the right time," I told myself. But as listening and sharing became a larger part of my life,

I realized there was something else at work here.

My students sensed instinctively what it took me years to comprehend.

FOUR CRUSHING LOSSES

We humans are handed many kinds of loss as we walk through life.

Loss of a Loved One

Loss of a loved one through death or divorce is experienced by all of us at one time or another, and thus it is the type of loss that we hear the most about. Since forty percent of the students in the college where I teach are over twenty-seven years old, this type of loss has touched many of their lives, and as our nation's baby boomers age, it's something common to almost everyone.

Loss of a Job

There are other types of losses, however, which are just as much a part of life as death and divorce. A common one is loss of one's job, whether it means dismissal from paid employment or a change of careers. As a result of the changing role of women, many women are making the shift from homemaker to employee. This shift is creating a loss that is being felt by many older women right now. While in college preparing for their new career, they become poignantly aware that they are losing a familiar job, which they feel comfortable with, for an uncertain future career.

Loss of a Role

An additional common loss being felt by many student/mothers in their forties is the loss of their role as caretaker mother. As these women watch their children grow into adulthood and leave home, they discover that being mother to an adult child means being needed in a totally new way. They mourn the loss of their former role while resenting the new role which has been thrust upon them.

Loss of Health

An additional loss which enters everyone's life is loss of health—our own or a loved one's. Strokes, heart attacks, cancer, arthritis, and the other diseases which plague mankind bring with them a loss of one's former activities, in essence, a loss of one's former self. Closely related to loss of health is loss of a part of one's body; amputation, mastectomy, and paraplegia bring losses which are both unique and similar to all the others.

Because all these losses have in them threads of similarity, anyone who has worked his way through the emotional roller coaster of one can relate to the same inner turmoil which is part of another. In varying degrees, all losses create anger, pain, sorrow, fear, and guilt. All frustrate us and temporarily immobilize us. All isolate us from the mainstream of life.

Because of the similarities that exist within all loss, I now know it's something other than chance or coincidence which causes people to reach out to me. I've been to hell and back, and those around me know it. It isn't as important to them that I've been there as it is that I got back. Instinctively they sense that I'm a survivor.

LOSS IS USUALLY UNEXPECTED AND UNWANTED

At nineteen, when my life was ripe with promise, I was in an automobile accident which severed my spine and paralyzed me from the chest down. Within seconds I made the transition from normal nineteen-year-old to paralyzed paraplegic. As most losses are, the transition was unexpected and unwanted.

Two Sundays before the wreck, wearing white high heels and a size-nine black cotton dress, I'd led the evening services at our church. It had been one of those hot, sultry August evenings when only a teenager would delight in dressing. I can still remember the heat of my "pre-air conditioning" bedroom as I looped white beads around my neck, clipped on matching earrings, and planned the evening ahead of me. The heat and humidity were totally insignificant at the time. On that particular day I was feeling especially good about myself and the person I was becoming. I vividly remember turning to check my reflection in the full-length mirror hanging on the back of my bedroom door and thinking, "You've got the world on a string. Everything's going your way." As I perched on the edge of adulthood, my world seemed perfect.

At that moment my world was perfect. I did indeed have "everything going my way." I was a junior in college, an honors student, and a leader in my church youth group. I was decent looking and popular; I had loving parents, numerous friends, and a secure environment. In short, my life held everything a nineteen-year-old could ask for.

Call it a twist of fate or irony of situation; two weeks later this girl who had everything going for her suddenly had next to nothing.

On Sunday, August 14, 1955, at 4:30 A.M., after having worked the night shift at my parents' ice cream store and sitting up half the night talking with the boy I was then dating, I sleepily climbed out of bed to bake a peach pie for the Youth Fellowship picnic. As I simultaneously dressed, baked, and put on make-up, I could hear the thunder rolling outside. Obviously, it was not exactly what one would call picnic weather, but, oblivious to the pelting rain, I grabbed the wicker basket, plopped in food, utensils, and the warm peach pie, kissed my mother good-bye, and set off down the street toward the church where we were to meet at 7:00 o'clock.

It was the last time my mother saw me walking.

Holding umbrellas, raincoats, and picnic baskets, members of our Youth Fellowship sat on the hoods of wet cars and briefly considered canceling the outing. After a few of us had convinced the others that "it probably isn't raining one hundred miles north of Muncie," we loaded the cars and headed for Pokagon State Park and an all-day outing. Although it was raining when we arrived, and continued to rain off and on most of the day, by afternoon the sun was shining brightly as we headed home. But the five of us in our car never got there.

On a dry, straight, two-lane highway in the middle of level Indiana farmland, our car and a car in the opposite lane crashed into each other. Our driver and the girl sitting behind him were killed instantly; two other friends, sitting on the far right side of the car, were left with permanent disabilities, and I, sitting in the middle of the back seat, had my life broken into so many pieces that I'm still trying to put it back together again.

HELP ME GET THROUGH THIS! HELP ME TO HEAL!

So when a person says to me, "You're the only one who understands," what he's really saying is, "You've been where I am. You've experienced this same hopelessness, bitterness, and frustration. But somehow you managed to get through it." The unstated plea is, "Help me get through it. Help me to find meaning in a life that seems totally meaningless. Help me to heal."

No one, of course, can ever heal someone else. When a person's life is lying shattered all around him, there is only one individual who can put it back together—the person himself. Nevertheless, picking up the pieces and rebuilding is a lot easier if the journey is made with someone who's already taken the trip.

While walking through my own valley of loss, and beside others going through theirs, I've discovered that finding meaning on the other side of the valley doesn't just happen by chance. We have to make it happen. Our ability to rebound depends to a large extent on our attitude toward the loss, coupled with the internal resources we have cultivated to deal with that loss.

It's not a question of whether or not life will deal us lousy hands. It will. The only question is how we will respond when it happens.

FALLING APART ISN'T AS EASY AS IT SOUNDS

*"Give sorrow words; the
grief that does not speak
Whispers the o'er fraught
heart and bids it break."*
Shakespeare,
MacBeth. IV, iii, 209

Before any healing can take place, we need to allow ourselves the luxury of falling apart. Only by fully experiencing our loss can we accept it, face it, and then move back into life again. This, however, is easier said than done.

DENIAL IS EASIER THAN FALLING APART

We are often the cause of our inability to fall apart. Because pain is an inherent part of loss, we try to avoid it at all costs, even pretending to ourselves and to the rest of the world that it doesn't exist. In an effort to protect ourselves from this ugly reality, without even being aware of what we're doing we go to great lengths devising ways to deny our feelings.

DENIAL OFTEN COMES CLOSE TO SELF-DESTRUCTION

After the wreck, I was inundated by losses, but the world saw me as having only one loss, the inability to use my legs. The question everyone was asking those first few days after the wreck was, "Will she ever walk again?" Everyone's attention was focused on "Barbara's loss": my inability to walk.

Whereas paralysis is just a word to most people, overnight it became a way of life for me, a way of life that brought with it more losses than the mind can comprehend. Within seconds, I lost my ability to walk, to run, to dance, to skate, to jog, even to stand. Society saw, and still sees, this inability to use my legs as my only loss.

For a short time I even got caught up in the lie of having only one loss, but as the weeks became months, and slowly turned into years, this inability to walk became a minor loss, almost superficial in light of all the others. Although it took me years to realize the scope and magnitude of all my losses, I knew almost immediately that I wanted nothing to do with them.

After coming out of a month-long coma and finding myself paralyzed, I was overwhelmed by what I wasn't able to do. I wasn't able to sit up by myself, turn over by myself, or dress myself. I wasn't even able to control my bowels or my bladder. It soon became painfully evident that I wasn't going to move like I used to move, act like I used to act, or look like I used to look. Even though I had not yet discovered all the harsh realities which were to hit me later, some corner of my mind instinctively knew I'd never be like I once was. There would be no more high heels, no more straight skirts, no more size nine dresses.

Barbara wouldn't be back, and this thing that had taken her place was a non-entity, a non-person. So slowly, but very systematically, I started to eliminate Barbara. She used to exist—before August 14, 1955— but she didn't exist now. I was determined this thing I had become was not me.

YOU'RE NOT A PERSON; YOU'RE A THING

I got through the first year following the wreck by carefully programming myself into believing that I wasn't a person; I was a thing.

Since ten of these first twelve months were spent in hospitals, my environment helped cushion me from reality. Nevertheless, my daily trips to physical therapy always brought a rude reminder of what I'd lost. Standing in braces at the end of the parallel bars, I'd hate the reflection I saw in the mirror. Staring back at me was a girl with a shaved head, wearing a bulky, chairback brace over a cotton T-shirt with no bra underneath; awkward, massive, long-leg braces (attached to size-ten brown tie oxfords); and formless cotton slacks. I would stare in disbelief: no hair, no make-up, no figure. Then I'd quickly remind myself that whatever that reflection was in the mirror, it wasn't me.

Because I would not allow myself to fall apart, five years of my life are blank pages filled only with pain and hopelessness. Although I breathed, talked, and seemed alive to the people around me, I ceased to exist between the ages of twenty and twenty-five. Since I couldn't accept the new me, I killed her.

It didn't matter, I told myself, that I'd never walk again, live again, or love again. It didn't matter because only people walked, lived, and loved. And I was no longer a person; I was a thing.

Every trip outside the house reminded me of my losses and reinforced my denial of my feelings. I'd be out shopping and see couples holding hands, obviously enjoying life and each other, and I'd remember all the times in the past when I'd been on dates, held hands, and felt wanted. I ached for what was no longer mine. These initial feelings of anger and jealousy, however, would quickly be repressed by reminding myself: "You're not a person; you're a thing."

This compound sentence became my litany for getting through every unbearable situation I faced. As long as I was not a person, I didn't have to participate in life again. By refusing to do so, I effectively excluded myself from the human race. However, I also effectively eliminated any opportunity to fall apart. But since then I've discovered I was far from alone.

STAYING TOGETHER FOR OTHERS

Recently after one of my classes had started a two-day discussion of "Paul's Case" (a short story dealing with a young boy's escapes from reality and ending with the ultimate escape, suicide), Melissa, a twenty-three-year-old woman, met me as I was heading back to my office. "I'm not coming to class tomorrow," she announced. "I wanted to tell you so you wouldn't think I was sick or something. I'll only be gone one day."

Knowing her brother had taken his own life only two years previously, I urged her to come in and talk. After we were in the office, I honestly expressed the ambivalence I always have about teaching that particular

21

short story. "I'm sorry about the lesson," I explained.
"Each year when I teach it, I find it has caused pain to
someone. Actually, I've thought about taking it out of
the syllabus, but it lends itself to such excellent class
discussion that I keep it. I know it had to open old
wounds for you, and I'm sorry."

Defiantly she assured me she had been untouched by
our discussion because, as she put it, she had already
"dealt with" her brother's death. Dry-eyed and in
total command of herself, she said, "I just don't want
or need to hear any more about suicide. I've read
enough about it to know what I want to know, and I
certainly don't think I'll gain a thing by hearing any
more talk." I assured her that missing the next class
was perfectly acceptable. "But are you sure you
know why you're skipping tomorrow?" I asked.

There's a Time for Tears

After a long silence she replied, "Yes, I do know. I
lied a minute ago. The discussion did cause memories, too many really. I had to fight tears all during
class today. It's just too hard on me. Although right
after Pete died I kept falling apart, crying at the
drop of a hat, I soon realized I had to pull myself
together if I were going to be any help to Mom and
Dad. I've not cried since the day of the funeral,
and I'm certainly not going to start now."

"I can see why you don't want to cry in front of your classmates," I assured her, "but crying is okay, you know. Tears aren't all bad." "No," she answered, "Crying is not okay. Mature people don't cry. Only little children cry." Although she skipped class the next day, she was back for the following lesson and dropped in often throughout the remainder of the year "just to talk."

The following September when I met Melissa in the hall, she happily told me she was now seeing a psychiatrist in an effort to penetrate the shield she had created to avoid grieving. "The pretending got to be too much," she confided. "I mean it was wearing me out. I was holding up for Mom and Dad, holding up for my sister, holding up for the public. The effort of holding myself together was just too much for me. When every other part of my life started falling apart, I knew I just couldn't keep on like I was. I finally saw that I needed help."

THE STRENGTH TRAP

This same type of denial of feelings occurred when Shawn, a thirty-nine-year-old woman, was suddenly confronted with widowhood. Less than a year after her husbands's unexpected death, at the urging of one of my former students, she had enrolled in my course.

After the quarter was well along, her friend dropped in my office for a visit. "How's Shawn doing?" she asked. "Very well," I replied, "but she'd do a lot better if she didn't miss so many classes. She seems to be sick a great deal." "No," Shawn's friend replied, "she's not really sick. Well, she's not physically sick. I mean, well, she's drinking too much. I know she is, and she knows she is; but she says it's the only way she can keep going."

Later, while talking privately with Shawn, I questioned whether she might have started college too soon after her husband's death. "Oh no," she answered, "Life must go on. I can't just sit around home and cry, you know. I've got to quit feeling sorry for myself and get my act together. Everyone keeps telling me that if I stay busy, I'll hurt less."

"Is it working?" I asked. Thoughtfully she replied, "Not at all. My whole life is an act. Each day I come to classes so people will think I'm handling Steve's death well, and then I go home and drink so I can face coming back to classes the next day. I'm in a trap." She told me how she was pulled between her own grief and her friends' insistence that she "get on with her life." Near the end of the quarter, realizing her trap was harming her, Shawn withdrew from college and started seeing a psychologist.

LIFE MUST GO ON—BUT NOT YET

Neither Melissa nor Shawn would allow herself to fall apart. Both were submerging their grief in order to be what they thought society wanted them to be. Both had been told that falling apart means weakness and that as mature people they should "hold themselves together" and "stay busy." Buying into the belief that "life must go on," they had skipped a necessary part of the mending process. They had ignored their feelings.

Most of us, like Melissa and Shawn, find it extremely difficult to deal with all the negative feelings that loss brings into our lives. Yet, we must understand and deal with them before we can go on.

A TIME FOR ANGER

Phyllis, a twenty-eight-year-old woman coping with an unwanted divorce, dealt with these negative feelings each time she had to talk with her ex-husband. When her guilt and anger would mount beyond her ability to deal with them, she'd be overwhelmed by feelings of inadequacy.

One night my phone rang. "I hate Bruce. This rejection is more than I can bear," said Phyllis. "When he came to pick up the kids this weekend, I stayed in the bedroom so I wouldn't have to talk to him. I knew that if I went out, I'd say things I'd later regret. I can spend the entire week trying to forget how much he hurt me, trying to get my pride back, and then, wham, he comes to get the kids, talks for only five minutes, and destroys the little bit of confidence I've spent all week getting."

"I don't like myself when I'm around him," she continued. "It's terrible to feel such hate toward someone who was my husband. I hate him for what he's doing to the kids, what he's doing to me. I hate him for having a nice car, when I have a junk heap; for having a new wife, when I have no one; for having money to buy steaks, when we live on macaroni and cheese. My friends tell me to get on with my life, but I can't. I wish I could. It sure would be a lot easier than having all these terrible feelings of anger and hate."

Of course it would be easier to "get on with life." Phyllis was ahead in the long run, however, by allowing herself to face her inner feelings, even when she didn't like what she saw. At this point, she really needed to fall apart, to admit her anger and hate, before she was ready to "get on with her life." Later, when Phyllis was ready, she did a beautiful job of healing, a job which could not have occurred if she had not admitted her feelings during the early stages of her loss.

THERE'S A TIME FOR FALLING APART AND "JUST FEELING"

Sherri, in her late thirties, was at this same point when she wrote an essay in my composition class about the pain of being a young widow. In one paragraph she said: "People don't really want to know how much I'm hurting. It's like I shouldn't still be sad, and if I am there must be something wrong with me. They'll say, 'It's been eight months now. Pull yourself together. Let's go out. We'll eat, mingle, and have some fun.' Good grief, I don't even want to eat, let alone mingle. Don't they realize I hurt all over? The emptiness I feel is taking over my reasoning. I can intellectually accept Greg's death, but all my wise reasoning flies to the wind when I look over and see that empty chair next to me at the breakfast table. Right now my pain is unbearable. My mind isn't functioning; I'm just feeling."

Although Sherri felt guilty because she couldn't "pull herself together," she was wise not to play games with herself just to please her friends' expectations. As painful as it is, there is a period after loss when it's healthy to just feel. Yet most people don't do it.

It's difficult to accept the fact that falling apart is a necessary step, a step which has to be taken before healing can take place. Although society tries to tell us differently, we need to remind ourselves that it's okay to hate what life has handed us, to consciously

27

feel the pain, anger, frustration, and unfairness that are an integral part of every loss. And most importantly, it's okay to have all these feelings without guilt. It's not only okay; it's necessary.

Denying Pain Is Russian Roulette

Whenever we deny our grief, regardless of the form that denial takes, all we're doing is hindering our chances of healing. Facing reality too soon is too painful. No one is able to immediately pick up the pieces of her broken life, and she shouldn't try. All she'll accomplish by doing so is make it that much harder on herself somewhere, sometime, a few years down the road.

Because the present is so painful, we devise ingenious ways to avoid admitting we are feeling sorrow, frustration, and anger. We long to turn back the hands of time to "before." Although we want desperately to go back to being our old selves, to having life like it was before the death, the divorce, the dismissal, we can't. And since we can never go back to being that person we were before the loss occurred, we have to create a new person, a new self. But doing so is impossible until we allow ourselves to grieve for that part of us that is gone. This doesn't mean we need to pour our pain over everyone around us. It does mean, however, that we should never lie to ourselves. Denying the pain of loss will only hurt us more in the end.

CONFRONTING SOCIETY

Unfortunately, society encourages us to play the game. Even though we want to fall apart, even though we need to fall apart, the public will do everything in its power to keep it from happening.

Two Popular Myths:

◆ Society says that every problem has a cure.

◆ Society says that all pain can be eliminated.

The public will not allow us to fall apart because we live in a society which believes that every problem has a cure. If you have a headache, take an aspirin; if you can't sleep, take a sleeping pill; if you're nervous, take a tranquilizer. We have convinced ourselves that all pain, be it physical or emotional, can be easily eliminated.

If pills won't solve the problem, other solutions are suggested. If you don't get good grades, study harder; if you can't get a good job, get more education; if you don't get that promotion, work longer hours. If more effort and education won't bring the solution, don't despair. Since every problem has a cure, find one. If your age is showing, have a face lift; if your day was stressful, have a drink; if it was unusually stressful, have three drinks.

BARRIERS WE HAVE TO HURDLE:

◆ Simple solutions and easy platitudes

◆ Unrealistic hope

◆ Refusal to look beyond the obvious

Since the emotional pain of loss does not have a cure, society doesn't know how to deal with it. People who want simple solutions for every problem in life become extremely uncomfortable when faced with the unknown, unresolved, and uncertain aspects of loss. When forced to deal with someone going through these aspects, they panic. As a result of this discomfort and panic, they search for soothing words to erase the pain, words which don't exist.

SIMPLE SOLUTIONS AND EASY PLATITUDES

Since there are no such magical words, they create easy answers. Ultimately, these attempts to give us instant relief are, at best, thoughtless and, at worst, cruel. Rather than comfort us, these easy answers only push our feelings deeper into hiding and actually hinder our ability to fall apart.

Of course no one deliberately hurts another person who's going through loss; on the contrary, people want very much to help. But too often they simply don't know how.

I can remember lying in the hospital on a Stryker frame for eight months, wearing a catheter, going to therapy, vomiting, coming back to my hospital room, being turned regularly like a piece of meat between two boards, staring at the floor for two hours, then the ceiling for two hours, hurting every time I moved—and then having some well-meaning person come in and tell me to count my blessings. I *was* counting, but the numbers kept getting jumbled by the catheters, the paralysis, and the pain.

Later, out of the hospital and dealing daily with denial, I was told repeatedly, "You're really very lucky. You've still got your arms and your mind." Although the statements were true, at the time I didn't feel lucky, and I deeply resented people's thinking I was. Did they have to sleep on four towels every night because they wet the bed? I did. Did they have to wear diapers and plastic pants each time they got dressed? I did. Did they have to worry constantly whether they smelled like urine? I did. Did they have to give themselves an enema every other day so their bowels would function smoothly? I did.

Verbal Band-aids Harm More Than They Help

Over and over, kind people wanted to magically

erase my emotional pain. Not knowing how, they would give me verbal band-aids. These people were totally unaware of the harm they were doing. At the very time in my life that I needed to mourn my current loss and to grieve for all my future losses, they were urging me not to do so. At the very time that I needed to express the anger and hate I felt toward the rotten deal life had handed me, they were implicitly reminding me, "Well-adjusted people don't stoop to anger and hate."

The public thought, and still thinks, that I made a smooth transition from being mobile to being paralyzed. I didn't. I hated what life had handed me, but for much too long I never admitted those feelings to myself or to those around me. I started submerging my resentment and pretending that "things really weren't so bad."

Doing so was a big mistake, but I did it because society had always seen me as a girl who believed that mature people, especially mature Christians, accepted willingly, even eagerly, whatever life handed them. I felt I had an image to protect, and protect it I did—to my own destruction. Everyone around me was saying, "My, isn't she handling it well." Little did they realize I was inwardly eroding with resentment and not in any way "handling it well." Rather, my life was a shaky facade built to fit what I thought society wanted me to be.

"I'm Sorry. It's Not Fair."

How much easier falling apart would be if people going through a significant loss could hear, "I'm sorry. It's not fair." These simple words are all the person going through loss wants or needs. Simple solutions and platitudes do nothing but create obstacles which make falling apart that much more difficult.

UNREALISTIC HOPE

An additional way that society hinders our ability to fall apart is by giving unrealistic hope. Because they want us to "pull ourselves together" and "get on with life" months, or even years, before we're emotionally ready, they refuse to allow us to grieve by urging us to forget the reality of the present.

This unrealistic hope sometimes comes from those closest to us. Because these are the ones who love us, they find it difficult to see us mourn.

You Won't Be Like You Used to Be

A few years ago I had a student who had been a paraplegic for only three years. When I first met Rhonda, she was weighted down with her own losses, as well as her mother's inability to allow her to express the resentment she was feeling toward them. Whenever Rhonda mentioned any of the frustration and anger she was experiencing, her mother quickly would assure her that this paralysis was only temporary and "doctors were going to have a cure any day now." The message being repeated was, "Don't cry; don't be angry; don't be disappointed. Soon you'll be like you used to be." But the message Rhonda was hearing was, "I can't accept you as you are."

Filled with frustration, she stopped by my office one day. "I wish Mother would quit cutting out every clipping she can find on spinal cord fusion," complained Rhonda. "She'll get all excited and tell me, 'See, someday you're going to walk again. Then you'll be just like everyone else.' Why can't she like me as I am, paralysis and all?" Poor Rhonda was caught between her need to work through her grief and her deep desire to please her mother.

By focusing all her attention on "a cure," her mother had short-circuited Rhonda's ability to mourn her losses and get on with life. As our talks became more frequent, Rhonda began to explore all the resentment she felt but didn't dare make known to her mother. Being a bright girl, she soon saw the harm being done by her mother's false hopes and started focusing on the pain she'd never been allowed to admit. It became quickly evident that in this case the daughter was more mature than the mother.

Things Will Be Different

Polly, a good-looking, twenty-eight-year-old woman who was dealing with an unwanted divorce, found that her mother was offering her the same type of unrealistic hope. Every time that Polly would show any signs of sadness over the loss of her marriage, her mother would quickly remind her that she'd "be married in a year." After one of these recurring confrontations, Polly called to tell me that enough was enough.

"Why," she said, "does Mother insist on thinking she can wipe away ten years of marriage with the promise that I'll marry again? In the first place, I don't want to be married in a year. In the second place, I don't think I'll ever want to be married again. I'm just sick and tired of her talking about marriage. Right now the last thing I even want to think about is getting married. All I want to do is learn to live with this pain, this emptiness. Why does she refuse to let me feel sad? It's like she'll give me a pill, the promise of a new marriage, and all the hurt will go away."

Conning Yourself

Part of my empathy for Rhonda and Polly resulted from my own experiences with unrealistic hope.

Soon after I was out of the coma, various nurses and doctors told me that I'd walk again. Although they were usually very careful to add a dependent clause such as "Even though you'll have to wear a brace and use crutches," the main idea was always there, always the same: "You'll walk again." Therefore, each time that I'd be on the tilt board, light-headed and vomiting, I'd remind myself that this was a necessary prelude to "walking again." After all, walking with a brace and crutch was not the end of the world, and what a wonderful change it would be from the life I was currently leading.

And then one fateful day in physical therapy I discovered what the nurses and doctors had really meant by "walking." While strapped to the tilt board, I got to watch a rehabilitated paraplegic walk. For the first time in my life I saw a person using two long-leg braces, a chairback brace, and Canadian crutches do what is called the swing-through step. When doing this step he let his paralyzed legs swing through the two Canadian crutches, regained his balance, moved the crutches forward, and repeated the process. As I watched this whole procedure, I fought tears, nearly choking as I attempted to hide my dismay. When I returned to the privacy of my hospital room, I cried until there were no more tears, only dry heaves. "No," my inner self screamed, "that's not walking."

And, of course, it isn't. It's a way of getting from here to there, but it's not walking. In an effort to keep me from falling apart, I had been purposely misled with half truths and false hope, and I resented it. It took me over three years to reject the braces and crutches in favor of life in a wheelchair, a decision I've never regretted, but one which came only after a great deal of emotional pain.

REFUSAL TO LOOK BEYOND THE OBVIOUS

Easy answers and unrealistic hope are not the only barriers society creates to keep us from falling apart; anyone whose loss has changed his looks is given an additional obstacle. Although all loss causes society discomfort, people find it unusually difficult to deal with a loss which changes one's physical appearance. I discovered this soon after leaving the hospital and entering the real world.

Without being aware of what they were doing, the public often reinforced my becoming a non-entity during the first years following the wreck. In the fifties it was unusual to find anyone leading an active, full life while living in a wheelchair. In fact, anyone seen in a wheelchair was treated as an invalid, a slightly-inferior, not-quite-normal individual. The words "confined to a wheelchair" carried with them a negative connotation which spilled over into people's attitudes and actions toward me and my loss.

Repeatedly when I was out in public, strangers treated me as if I didn't exist, holding an animated conversation with the person accompanying me, carefully avoiding looking at me or, heaven forbid, including me in the conversation.

I vividly remember shopping in a large department store in Ft. Wayne and having a clerk, with me sitting right beside her examining dresses on a rack, ask my father, "What type of dress is she looking for?" Although my father knew exactly the type of dress I was hunting, he directed the question away from himself, thereby forcing the clerk to deal with me on a one-to-one basis.

A similar situation occurred while my mother and I were waiting for the elevator in an Indianapolis department store. An older woman standing near us started questioning Mother about me, oblivious to the fact that I was sitting only inches from her. She opened the conversation by asking, "What in the world happened to the poor, dear girl?" In an effort to terminate the interrogation, Mother replied simply, "Oh, she was in a wreck a few years ago." Continuing to talk about me in third person as if I weren't present, the woman asked, "Was her mind affected?" to which Mother, with her typical quick thinking, retorted, "No, and neither was her hearing."

Society's platitudes, easy answers, and unrealistic hope hinder a person's ability to see himself as a significant person capable of having significant losses, and inevitably, the denial process begins: "I'm not a person; I'm a thing."

WE MUST ALLOW
OURSELVES TO FALL APART

Grief is very much a part of every loss, and when we deny that fact we retard our chances to work through the healing process. Although society encourages us to believe differently, denial of loss is not a cure; it's only a placebo.

Immediately following a loss, we desperately need denial in order to protect ourselves from a reality whose weight would crush us. Denial at that time becomes for us an effective way of avoiding unbearable pain. Nevertheless, it can, like most things in life, become destructive when carried to excess. Sooner or later (how soon or how late is an individual matter) we must allow ourselves to mourn our loss, cry our sorrow, vent our anger, and face our resentment. We need to admit to ourselves that the loss isn't fair, isn't just, and we detest it. Eventually, we must allow ourselves to fall apart; it's the only way we'll ever be able to put ourselves back together again.

WE ARE NOT LEAVES
IN THE WIND

*"Circumstances are beyond
the control of man; but
his conduct is in his own
power."*

Benjamin Disraeli,
Contarini Fleming

After allowing ourselves to fall apart, we slowly discover we're ready to face reality, walk through loss, and find wholeness again. However, this process occurs only if, and when, we want it to occur. We, and we alone, make the choice: to face reality, or hide from it; to walk through loss, or wallow in it; to create wholeness, or live in a meaningless void.

WALKING THROUGH LOSS IS
A PRIVATE JOURNEY

Once we've gotten around our denial and come face to face with our feelings, inevitably we're going to become overwhelmed by hopelessness. We'll wonder if we're ever going to feel normal again, and we find ourselves asking, "Will this pain go on year after year?" "Will life always be this empty?" And for weeks, months, and even years, we're sure that the answer is "Yes."

The well-known phrase "Life is not fair" suddenly takes on profound significance. What was once only a much-repeated cliche now becomes a personal truth. Life, of course, is not fair; it never has been and it never will be. Nevertheless, each of us has a choice. We can spend the remainder of our lives banging our head against life's injustices, or we can accept them as an inherent part of the human condition and move on.

RUNNING FROM REALITY IS EASIER THAN WALKING THROUGH LOSS

Moving on, however, is so painful that many of us decide it just isn't worth the effort. We discover it's much easier to sit in our own private self-pity than to actively take responsibility for our own healing. Rather than face the pain and walk through it, most of us spend months running from reality. And it doesn't take us very long to discover that society makes our running easy, constantly encouraging us to "get out of the house" and "keep busy." Although these suggestions are meant to keep us from the clutches of self-pity, in essence they become escape hatches for people already searching for ways to avoid reality.

Three Ways We Run from Reality

◆ Anesthetize our feelings

◆ Shift responsibility to someone else

◆ Decide we're a victim of circumstance

WE ANESTHETIZE OUR FEELINGS

When we tell a recently divorced person to "get out of the house and meet people," what we may very well discover is that she or he slips easily into the readily available life of singles' bars and casual one-night stands. Both alcohol and sex become terribly attractive opiates when a person is face to face with loss. In its own way each anesthetizes the pain of having to take responsibility for one's own healing.

Alcohol, the Escape Hatch

Diane was thirty-six years old when her husband walked out of her life. Although the divorce settlement left her and their four children in financially good condition, Diane was emotionally devastated by her husband's new attitude and lifestyle. Even though he regularly sent the more-than-adequate child support payments, he had dropped completely out of their life, going months without seeing or contacting them. Concerned about the effect his rejection was having on the children, Diane found herself trying to be both mother and father. Hours she usually would have spent alone were now spent with her children. No longer did she feel free to shut the bedroom door while studying, do the grocery shopping by herself, or even go next door to visit. In the process, she was filled with frustration as her own life became totally child-centered.

She told me that when she first accepted a friend's offer to go to a popular singles' bar, her only reason was "to get out of the house" and have a "relaxing evening away from the children." That relaxing evening was to be the beginning of two years of weekly bar-hopping.

As she later told me, "It was wonderful at first. After spending a week doing nothing more stimulating than sorting socks, packing lunches, and settling arguments, it was marvelous to be around adults. After a drink or two I found that my problems at home seemed less catastrophic; after three or four, I was sure that I could handle anything that came my way. It was just amazing the way I could swish away all the mutterings in my mind once I'd had a few drinks. But then I started liking that euphoric feeling so much that my customary two drinks gradually became six. I'd be so out of it by the time I got home that I'd swear, 'Never again!' Nevertheless, when the next Friday night rolled around, I'd be right back, rationalizing that I deserved at least one night a week for myself."

The Sexual Merry-Go-Round

Peggy, twenty-eight years old and recently divorced, also found temporary comfort in a singles' lounge, but unlike Diane, she seldom went home. Instead, she spent the night at "his house"—with the "his" changing every few months. She and Diane were similar in that their divorces had left them filled with frustration, but different in that while Diane had adequate income, Peggy didn't know how she'd buy next week's groceries. The child-support payments were never on time, usually nonexistent, and always inadequate. One day while sitting in my office she explained how her divorce had caused her to doubt her self-worth: "We were broke, as usual, and I was feeling like everything was my fault. I mean if I'd been prettier or sexier—or something—Jeff wouldn't have left me for that young thing he's living with now. As I look back, I think that I started going to the singles' lounge sort of as a test of myself. I felt like a twenty-eight-year-old loser, and I desperately wanted reassurance that I wasn't."

She stopped to make sure I was understanding, and

then continued, "At first it was super. Because I'm a rather good dancer, the men quickly paid attention to me. I felt like a person again, like a desirable woman, rather than just a jilted wife. But the truth is that everyone there was on the prowl, and it wasn't very long before I began feeling more like a piece of meat than a person."

Peggy shifted the pile of books on her lap, stared at the wall above my head, and said, "But the odd part is that I continued to go. It just didn't make sense. It was almost like an addiction. I'd pretend I was going because I enjoyed dancing, but deep down inside I knew I wanted what came after the music stopped. It became a weekly ritual: dance a lot, flirt a little, and always end up in bed. I wanted so much to be held, to feel desired, that I'd have sex just to feel a man's arms around me, his body close to mine. I craved to be wanted again, not for just a night, but forever."

Although Peggy rode this sexual merry-go-round for nearly three years, the gold ring always eluded her. Every few months I'd get a phone call from her announcing: "This time is different. This is really it." But it never was.

The Escape Clause

I've watched many people get stuck in escapes for years before discovering that, as tantalizing as they first seemed, they didn't solve problems or eliminate grief. In fact, they often increased them. Although these escapes seemed like magic solutions as they temporarily numbed the pain, when their effects wore off, the pain was still there staring them in the face. By their very nature these escapes demanded more of the same. Because of this, what was initially sought as a harmless escape from a problem in time became a problem in and of itself.

SHIFTING RESPONSIBILITY TO SOMEONE ELSE

Another common way to run from reality and avoid the pain of doing our own healing is to shift the responsibility for our life onto someone else. When going through a significant loss, we often beg others to tell us how to act, what to say, where to go—even what to wear and eat. We try to distance ourselves from the emotional pain by handing our life and all its decisions to someone else.

Going Back to Mother

Denise fell into this trap and found it short-circuited her healing process for over two years. When I met her, she was only beginning to see that she had helped create many of her own problems. After her divorce, this good-looking, forty-year-old woman had abdicated all responsibility concerning her life. She had let her mother, a sixty-year-old widow who was overly anxious to help, buy the groceries, cook the meals, babysit the children, and pay the bills. For months following her divorce, Denise complacently let her mother run her life. When Mother decided their house was too big, they moved into an apartment; when Mother decided parochial school was too expensive, the children were transferred to public schools; when Mother decided their car was too old, they bought a new one.

One afternoon nearly three years after her divorce, Denise came into my office and announced, "My life is not my own. I live in an apartment that's too small, send my kids to a school I don't like, and drive a car I can't afford. I've lost all control of my life."

The Easy Out

It's extremely easy to use this route of escape. We don't want to make decisions. We're tired. We hurt. Because there have been too many changes in too short a time, life is confusing, and we find it easy to escape reality. What we really want is for someone else to do our work for us, work that only we can do. Although this transferral of responsibility may be helpful for a short time, eventually, like Denise, we discover that it won't solve our problems. Even while our outer voice urges others to run our life and insulate us from reality, our inner self screams, "Leave me alone." This ambivalence unbalances our lives and, more importantly, it immobilizes us so we can't go forward and get on with living.

It's Our Journey

It's true that the trip through loss is easier if we have people standing on the sidelines cheering us on; however, we must never forget that although friends and family can stand beside us, we alone must do the walking.

Each step back to wholeness is a solitary, private step, and no one can take these steps for us because the changes taking place are internal.

CHOOSING TO BE A VICTIM OF CIRCUMSTANCE

In many cases we don't want to take those steps. In an effort to avoid them, we manufacture the clever rationalization that we're victims of circumstance and as such have no responsibility for our own healing.

As the frustration and grief of loss increase, we lash out at life. We feel like puppets—with someone else out there pulling the strings. We constantly remind ourselves that this loss was not our idea; we didn't ask for it, and we certainly don't deserve it. It was handed to us by forces beyond our control, and since it was given to us against our will, why should we have to heal ourselves? At times like these, it's much easier to play the victim than to take responsibility for managing our own lives.

A Personal Choice

Blaming something outside ourselves for all the ripples of sorrow that come from loss is as natural as breathing. I know it was amazingly easy for me to blame all my problems on the wreck. My thinking went like this: "I can't help it if I'm bitter. I have every right in the world to be depressed and angry. You see I was in a wreck which severed my spinal cord and left me paralyzed for the rest of my life. I didn't choose this rotten life; I'm a victim of circumstances. I planned on being happily married, having delightful children, and creating a loving family. Don't you see? The wreck ruined my life."

CIRCUMSTANCES CAN STEAL FREEDOM

In moments of helplessness and frustration, I found it was terribly easy to fall into this victim mentality. This was especially true as I faced the fact that I'd lost all freedom to do the simple tasks which are a part of daily living.

Losing Control of Our Environment

I hated the fact that objects could no longer be easily carried, picked up, or moved, and resented the circumstances which had put these limitations on me. Carrying anything became an adventure in itself. Needing both hands free to move my wheelchair, I had to transport everything on my lap. A weekly task as simple as carrying out the trash suddenly was a major ordeal as I'd carefully balance the slippery Hefty bag on my lap, clamp my teeth on one end of it so it wouldn't slide, and head for the curb. This carrying things on my lap brought constant problems: ice cubes melted, coffee spilled, casseroles tipped, hot dishes burned, papers slid. My frustration mounted and grew. Even though I had reachers and a short-handled mop, it didn't take long to discover that all the "tools for the handicapped" in existence couldn't lessen the feeling of helplessness that came over me as I watched numerous ice cubes scatter on the kitchen floor, lodging in the most inconvenient corners possible, or saw the wind blow a stack of just-graded essays under the bed. The once simple task of picking up these scattered items was now always difficult—and often impossible.

I soon discovered, however, that while this inability to easily carry and pick up objects caused frustration, it was insignificant compared to the helplessness of not being able to make my body do what

I wanted it to. Whereas I carried items only a few times each day and dropped them even less frequently, my inability to move my own body was an hourly frustration. This helplessness mounted as it became painfully evident that simple things like getting in and out of bed, off and on the toilet, and in and out of the car were skills which had to be learned again from scratch. Something as common and easy as turning over in bed was now a major production. Even something as simple as sewing caused frustration. As I sat there awkwardly controlling the foot-feed with my forearm while simultaneously guiding the material through the pressure foot, I became immensely resentful.

Losing Control of Our Futures

Life had trapped me, stripping away all my freedom. I found I was at the mercy of my spinal cord, and I hated it. I soon discovered, however, that although this inability to make my body do what I wanted was frustrating, that frustration was not to be my major loss.

Within a very short time after the wreck, I became painfully aware that my biggest loss was that marriage would not be a part of my future. In my early twenties, the agony of realizing a man would never hold, cuddle, or desire me again was unbearable. The thought of going through life alone—unloved, unneeded, and unwanted—made all my other losses seem insignificant. As I watched my friends marry, start homes, and have children, I saw them entering a significant segment of life that was being denied to me. At moments like these, it was easy to consider myself a hopeless victim of circumstance.

WE ARE NOT LEAVES IN THE WIND

Time and experience have shown me that we are not victims of circumstance. Although forces outside ourselves play a significant role in our lives, they do not control us. I'm convinced that we're destroyed not so much by forces outside ourselves as by forces within. I believe that you and I give direction to our lives by the choices we make and the attitudes we have.

The specific circumstance that comes into a person's life is not as significant as that person's reaction to it.

We Choose How We Will Respond to Loss

Even though unwanted loss comes into everyone's life, each of us chooses how to respond to that loss. After we have ached with anguish, cried until no more tears will come, and hated the world and everything in it, there comes a point in our lives when we must choose how we're going to respond to what life has handed us.

We choose to face reality—or evade it, to accept our loss—or hide from it, to grow stronger—or remain emotionally crippled. We decide if the loss is going to control us, or if we are going to control the loss. Once we accept the reality that we have a choice, we've taken a giant step toward wholeness.

Thus, only for a limited amount of time are we actually victims of circumstance. Victor Frankl realizes this when he says in *Man's Search for Meaning:* "To be sure a human being is a finite being, and his freedom is restricted. It is not freedom from conditions, but freedom to take a stand toward conditions." Moment by moment we choose how we are going to handle the loss which has entered our lives, and we cease to be victims of circumstance once we accept the fact that at any given moment we can modify our attitudes and alter our choices.

OUR ATTITUDES DETERMINE OUR DESTINY

Circumstances, in and of themselves, do not determine our destiny; to a large extent, we determine our own destiny by our attitude toward those circumstances.

Ceasing to think of myself as a victim was a turning point in my own life. Although it had taken me far too long to fall apart, once I did, I became acutely aware that I, and I alone, was responsible for my own attitude and thus for my own healing. Only when I came to this realization was I able to face reality and start that long, slow walk through loss. Only then was I able to admit openly to myself and to those around me that I detested being paralyzed. Only then was I able to say, "Okay. Life has handed me a rotten deal. It isn't fair and it isn't just; I did nothing to cause it and I certainly don't deserve it. But facts are facts. I'm paralyzed. Now what am I going to do about it? What am I going to do to make life meaningful for myself and for those around me?"

Refocusing

This step of facing reality changed the focus of my life. As I searched for ways to respond to what life had handed me, I found a new level of meaning in the words of the psalm: "Yea though I walk through the valley of the shadow of death, I will fear no evil." I noticed for the first time that the psalmist doesn't say, "Yea though I'm *in* the valley"; he says, "Yea though I walk *through* the valley." The difference in those two prepositions changed the direction of my life.

I realized I had to focus my energy on "walking *through*" my loss, rather than being consumed by the loss itself. I comprehended with a new clarity that if I concentrated my time and energy on self-pity, I'd end up staying in the valley forever. Only by changing my attitude would I ever begin to heal.

We Are Responsible for Our Own Healing

This idea that we are responsible for our own healing makes many people uncomfortable. These are the people who would much rather think of themselves as passive receivers of rotten circumstances than admit that they are responsible for their own lives. These are the same people who have great difficulty dealing not only with their own losses but with ours as well.

TIME DOESN'T HEAL US: WE HEAL OURSELVES

Rather than help us work through our emotional pain, we are often handed the over-used band-aid: "Time Heals," implying that if we just keep breathing long enough our sorrow and grief will vanish. Nonsense. I've watched too many people walk through loss to accept the idea that "time heals." The more accurate statement is "time numbs."

Although time and distance cause the sharp edges of our pain to be softened, they do not heal us. No matter how many months pass, no matter how many miles we move, loss does not go away. Whether we've lost a person, a job, our health, or part of our body, that loss is real. The divorced mate will not return, the lost job will not be given back, the arthritic joints will not disappear, the paralyzed legs will not move. A part of our life is gone, over, never to return. Since our healing is not assured nor automatic, sitting around waiting for time to heal us is futile.

And this healing is more likely to begin once we realize that meaning after loss doesn't just happen by chance; we have to make it happen.

WE HAVE THE POWER TO CULTIVATE OUR INTERNAL RESOURCES

We've all seen the same kind of loss devastate one person while making another stronger, and we've all asked why some people successfully put the pieces back together while others stay shattered. I believe the secret is the development of inner resources. The potential for a meaningful life is within each of us, but these internal seeds won't mature unless we want them to. We set our priorities in life, and our choices and attitudes grow out of those priorities. As a result, we deliberately cultivate our internal resources; they don't just magically appear in our hour of need. Although there are many intangibles which weave themselves together to make a person whole again, I've discovered that the key difference between the person who successfully heals and the one who doesn't is the development of these resources.

Can a fragmented person be put back together? Can he ever be whole again? Can he ever live a meaningful life? In short, is there life after loss? The answer is "Yes." But it's a qualified yes.

We will heal only if we realize that putting ourselves back together is our own responsibility and demands we focus on what's within us, not without. Meaning after loss is a by-product of our attitudes and our choices. The seeds of this meaning are internal, not external, and the person who develops these internal resources can find the strength to pick up the pieces of her broken life and again become a complete person.

FIVE INTERNAL RESOURCES

Okay, you're saying. I'm broken. You don't have to convince me. I've gone through all the stages you've mentioned. I've devised ways to deny my feelings, and I've refused to let myself fall apart, but finally there came a time when I said to myself, "No. This denial is not healthy and I'm ready to move on." I've moved beyond society's pat platitudes, simple solutions, and unrealistic hope.

And now I see that I'm ready. I'm ready to face reality, to walk through loss, and to mend myself. But how do I do it?

One Step at a Time

PREPARATION STEP: Accept the fact that we do have control over our own destiny. Accept the fact that circumstances, in and of themselves, are not as significant as our attitude toward those circumstances. By accepting this fact that we have control over our attitude, choices, and priorities, we find ourselves ready and able to mend.

There are five intangible, internal resources which when developed will make it easier for each of us to walk successfully through a loss.

1. **Believe in Your Own Uniqueness**
   The foundation for all other internal resources is the belief that each individual is unique and valuable. We need to affirm that life does indeed have a pattern and determine how we fit into that total mosaic.

2. **Discover That Success Is Intangible**
   Loss forces us to shift our values and redefine success. Healing occurs when we discover that it is what we *are*, not what we have, that makes us successful.

3. **Listen With Love**
   We can move out of the me-centeredness of loss by losing ourselves in the needs of those around us. By giving away our energy, time, and attention, we discover that our own pain diminishes.

4. **Live Life In Small Slices**
   By living "in" the moment, and not living "for" the moment, we find we can lessen the fear of the future and the pain of the past.

5. **Invest In Solitude**
   All of our internal resources are cultivated in these quiet moments we spend alone getting acquainted with our inner self. By taking the risks of aloneness, we discover new strength to meet life with all its inherent losses, present and future.

In the chapters that follow, I explain these resources fully, to help anyone broken by loss begin to heal himself.

HEALING

4

BELIEVING IN YOUR OWN UNIQUENESS

> *"It is not what he has, nor even what he does, which directly expresses the worth of a man, but what he is."*
>
> Henri-Frederic Amiel,
> *Journal*

Loss has a way of forcing us to examine life. Even if we've never previously given much thought to life's purpose or plan, once a significant loss enters our lives, we find ourselves asking, "What's it all about?" We start relentlessly searching for answers to questions which the rest of the world ignores or sweeps under the rug.

Life, we decide, should make some kind of sense. It becomes very important to us that this emotional pain we're going through fit into some kind of a pattern.

WHAT'S IT ALL ABOUT?

Discovering what gives life meaning is a difficult task whether it's immediately following a loss or years later. All of us have days, even months, in which we, like Thoreau, lead lives of "quiet desperation," but for many of us experiencing a loss, this state of mind becomes a way of life. Our society has so thoroughly programmed us for instant gratification that we find it difficult to look beyond the pain of the moment. But look beyond it we must. By looking beyond our present loss and standing outside our immediate grief, we're able to take the first, faltering steps in the healing process. We're able to ask, and ultimately answer, the question, "What makes life worth living?"

Not Having All the Answers Is Okay

Most of us find this a very difficult step to take. Although we may be tempted now and then to grapple with the meaning of existence, few of us actually do it. Although we want to develop our own personal theology and find our place in life's pattern, we discover the pain of facing those unanswerable questions is just too great.

As long as life is predictable and placid, most of us manage to anesthetize ourselves against these disturbing questions. For most of us, only the jar of a significant loss will pull us from our anesthetized fog.

WHAT MAKES LIFE
WORTH LIVING?

Getting through present pain can be made easier if we believe three powerful statements. These statements become three steps for discovering what makes life worth living.

First Step: I Have a
Theology of Life

After loss, we feel a need to reaffirm or develop our own personal theology of life. When we do so, we form the foundation for all our other internal resources. By getting in touch with our spiritual core, we find the strength to rebuild our shattered life.

The spiritual core within me at the time of the wreck is the same one that is within me today. I believe that God is Love and I am a channel for that Love. As a channel for a power that is stronger than death, divorce, illness, or paralysis, I have value and my life has meaning.

At this moment, you may have a clear idea of your own personal theology of life, and it may very well be different than mine. This does not lessen its importance.

Second Step: Life Has a Pattern

Regardless of your or my individual religious beliefs, we have one thing in common: each of us is a tiny

piece in the mosaic of life. Before we can successfully walk through a loss, we need to affirm that life
does indeed have a pattern and determine how we fit
into the total picture.

One of the few good things about loss is that it forces
us to get acquainted with our inner selves. In the
process, we form attitudes toward our own worth.
These attitudes are then reflected in every corner of
our lives.

If I see myself as being an important part of life's
pattern, that attitude will spill over into the lives of
others; on the contrary, if I see no sense in my being
alive, that too will influence every life I touch. If I
don't love myself, I'll never be able to love others; if
I don't trust myself, inevitably I won't be able to trust
those around me. The way I value the world will be a
reflection of the way I value myself. And the way I
value myself will be a reflection of my relationship
with God.

Third Step: I am a Valuable
Piece in Life's Pattern

The belief that each of us is unique and valuable
forms the foundation for all our other internal resources. Only with an awareness that we have something special to give the world, something uniquely
ours, something of value, will we be willing to invest

the time and energy needed to pick up the pieces of our life and move on.

When life is going smoothly and loss is a million miles away, it's fairly easy to say, "I'm a unique piece in life's pattern." It's often a very different story, however, when loss is standing on our doorstep. Suddenly we aren't at all sure that life even has a pattern, let alone that we have a special place in it. More likely, life seems senseless, and our place in it meaningless. These are the times when it's difficult to believe in any theology, let alone in ourselves. Yet these are the very times when we most need to believe.

If, before a loss occurs, we have already formed our spiritual foundation, we will discover it holds while everything around us crumbles. In it we will find the strength to look beyond the emotional pain of the moment to the overall pattern of life—and find that pattern to be good. In the process we'll discover that loss doesn't erase a person's unique place in that pattern. I found this to be true in my own life.

LOSS DOESN'T ERASE A PERSON'S UNIQUENESS

After six difficult years filled with hopelessness and helplessness, I began once again to see myself as a significant piece in life's pattern.

Because loss had left its many emotional scars, I discovered that I was now a different person than I had been six years earlier. Although I'd spent these years immediately following the wreck attempting to separate myself from this new person I had become, slowly I began to realize that although changed, I was still valuable. With that realization, I re-entered the human race, deciding that part of my re-entry would include a return to college.

Re-entering the Human Race

This return became a rite of passage as I picked up the fragments of myself and slipped back into the total mosaic of life.

That First Small Step

Going back to college as a junior in 1961 was nothing like going as a freshman in 1953. I was eight years older, in a wheelchair, and totally unsure of my abilities. Adding to my insecurity was the fact that I had changed my major from home economics to English, an outward statement of a significant shift in my goals and dreams.

Although I had known a degree in home economics would eventually give me financial independence, I hadn't chosen the field for that reason. I had chosen it because I wanted to be an effective homemaker.

As a result of the feminist movement of the '70s, the word "homemaker" now carries negative connotations, but in the '50s it was still acceptable, even desirable, for a woman to make her home the center of her life. Because I believed I could make the world a better place by being a good wife and mother, I had started college as a home economics major. Being reared in a home filled with love and discipline, I had wanted nothing more than to create a replica of it in my own future. Therefore my change of majors was much more than simply switching from home economics to English; it signaled the death of a dream. And at nineteen, dreams die hard.

At age twenty-six, I found myself sitting in English classes with seventeen-year-olds all around me. I felt antiquated and overwhelmed. Convinced that I could never compete with their fresh young minds, I experienced a self-imposed pressure to excel such as I had never known in my life.

The Challenge of Going On

In an effort to help me catch up with the other English majors, my advisor gave me a schedule that would have been refused by any seasoned English student, but which I, being naive and innocent, accepted. Unaware that I was facing one of the most difficult quarters of my academic life, I plunged ahead.

With the advantage of hindsight, I can see that my

first year back was "trial by fire." After the alarm jarred me awake at 4:00 A.M., I'd sit in the silent predawn hours furiously studying new material and reviewing old, spend the remainder of the day rotating between classes and study, and drop exhausted into bed at night, only to repeat the grueling process the following day.

It was demanding, it was draining, and at the same time it was one of the most exhilarating years of my life.

Once Again in the Game

Something marvelous happened. For the first time in six years, I had a reason to get out of bed in the morning; for the first time in six years, I had a goal.

No longer was I the shapeless glob which had stared back at me from the end of the parallel bars in physical therapy. Although I felt this new identity taking shape inside me, I feared it was just an internal illusion—just me fooling myself. My first hint that others were seeing the change came when one of the hometown papers did a human interest story concerning my return to college. Reading the article and looking at the pictures, I thought, "I'm a person again. No more leg braces; no more shaved head; no more maternity tops. Society sees me as a real person."

After over six years of sitting on the sidelines of life, I was once again a participant.

OVERCOMING LOW SELF-ESTEEM

For a period following a loss, all of us sit on the sidelines, not because we want to, but because it's a necessary part of picking up the pieces of our shattered life. Making the step from spectator to participant doesn't come easily for anyone, but it is more difficult for some than for others.

It is especially difficult for anyone whose identity has been an integral part of what (or whom) she has lost. For example, the woman who has always seen herself only as "Joe's wife" will have a hard time believing she has any value once "Joe" is gone.

Pamela was forty-one-years old when her husband died. When she walked into my classroom one September day, she brought with her a mountain of insecurity. As the year progressed, I watched that insecurity vanish as she discovered for the first time that she was a person in her own right, that she had an identity outside that of being her husband's wife.

Soon after the quarter began, she called my home one night crying. "I'm going to drop your class. I really have enjoyed these two weeks with you, but

I'm just not college material. I want you to know that it's not because of you; it's just that I'm not smart enough." Knowing that most older adults panic when first returning to school, I urged her to come in the next day and talk about her decision.

The next day this good-looking, well-dressed woman settled into the chair beside me, and I could feel her nervousness. Trying to calm her, I said, "Relax, Pamela. Forget I'm your teacher for a few minutes. We're nearly the same age. Let's just be friends for a while and get to know each other."

"Oh, we could never be friends," was her instant reply. "I'm dumb and uneducated and you're smart and have college degrees." It didn't take long to see that her low self-esteem came from being married for over twenty years to a man who had kept her totally dependent on him. He had repeatedly reminded her that she hadn't finished high school and wasn't smart enough to understand the world around her.

At the time of her husband's death, Pamela had never paid a bill, written a check, or balanced a checkbook. She had no idea what insurance policies they owned or what taxes they paid. She didn't know how much their monthly mortgage payments were or how much money they had in savings. Naturally, after her husband's death Pamela was left in chaos, and his words seemed like a prophecy to her: "You're not smart enough to understand the world around you."

Sitting beside me, she reviewed the last few years of her life: "Even though I finally did learn to handle the financial affairs, I always heard in the back of my mind, 'You're too dumb to understand. You didn't even finish high school.' Because I wanted to be a registered nurse, I finally got up the nerve to go back and get my GED, and with my cousin's encouragement I enrolled here and was accepted in the nursing program.

"But now that I'm actually here, I'm having a lot of doubts about whether it was the smart thing to do. That's why I'm dropping your class. I guess I'm so afraid of failing that I'd rather withdraw. I'm not very smart, you know."

A Fear—Not a Fact

Realizing that not being smart was a fear, rather than a fact, I encouraged her to stick with me, even if it were just for a few more weeks. She took my suggestion, staying not just for a few more weeks, but for the entire year, getting A's each quarter, and becoming an R.N. four years later at a ceremony where she was recognized as one of the outstanding students in her graduating class.

"I'm a nurse," she joyously told me. "It took me four years, but look at me now! For the first time in my life I feel as if I'm worth something."

BELIEVING IN YOUR OWN UNIQUENESS GIVES YOU THE STRENGTH TO PICK UP THE PIECES

I've watched many students like Pamela take that giant step from spectator to participant, and in the process of taking it they've come to believe in themselves strongly enough to counteract a society which often scoffs at the idea of individual uniqueness. These students are inevitably surprised to discover that I understand the difficulty involved in picking up the pieces of a broken life and finding one's place in life's pattern. I understand because I've been there.

In the '50s there were few people in wheelchairs who actively participated in life, and the vast majority of those who did were either secretaries or accountants. In the eyes of everyone who knew me, my future was virtually determined. Since my parents had an accounting firm already established at the time of my accident, people naturally assumed that I'd be an accountant. The script they had written for my life had me getting my degree in accounting and working happily ever after in my parents' office. This script seemed too good to be true—and it was.

Although others saw this as the sensible scenario for my life, they ignored one small problem: I detested accounting. I'd worked enough in the field to know

74

that I didn't want to spend the remainder of my life with ledgers, journals, and balance sheets. Knowing that I was too much a people-person to be happy working with numbers, I announced to the world that I wanted to be a teacher. The world then replied that I must be out of my mind.

Every way I turned someone was telling me how risky my decision was and urging me not to gamble with my life. My teachers, advisors, and rehabilitation counselor all told me that accounting would be a much safer profession.

Later I discovered the cause of their concern: Indiana had never licensed a person in a wheelchair to be a teacher.

All the Difference

I, like thousands of students before me, had to choose between a career that was safe and one that was satisfying. Living in a society which advocates safety above all else, I found it to be a difficult decision; however, with my parents' blessing, I, like Frost, took "the road less traveled" and "that has made all the difference." Because of my belief in my own uniqueness, I was the first person in a wheelchair to be licensed to teach in the state of Indiana. But much more importantly, because of my belief in my own uniqueness, I'm now in a profession which I thoroughly enjoy.

BELIEVING IN YOUR OWN UNIQUENESS GIVES YOU THE STRENGTH TO KEEP POUNDING ON LIFE'S CLOSED DOORS

Being licensed to teach, however, and actually teaching are two entirely different things, and the next eight years of my life were to be filled with professional rejections, rejections that shattered my world—and almost shattered me. Only my strong conviction that teaching was to be my thread in the fabric of life held me together.

Strike One

My first round with professional rejection came the year I finished college and was refused a job solely because I was handicapped.

When I returned to school, my father's wise advice was, "Learn to do something better than most people can do it, and someone will hire you." With that in mind, I gave college everything I had. At the time it all seemed so logical, so simple. If I could only prove to some principal that I was better qualified than his other applicants, naturally he'd hire me. After finishing all the course work for my bachelor's degree, getting through student teaching with flying colors, and completing my master's degree on a teaching assistantship, I came face to face with a miracle, or so I thought.

A high school English chairman, who had watched me teach numerous times, wanted to hire me. I was filled with excitement as I completed applications, photocopied resumes, and waited for what I was sure would be my first job offer. "Ah, there really is justice in the world after all," I rejoiced. "Someone wants me! All my hard work is going to pay off." My elation came to an abrupt end one May evening when the chairman came to my home with the news that his recommendation and my application had been turned down. "We don't want a crippled woman on our faculty," had been the superintendent's response.

Knowing the kindness the chairman was showing me (rejections come in crisp, form letters, not via kind, personal home visits), I managed to keep my composure until he walked out our front door. Only then did I let myself acknowledge the shattering pain inside me as I went into my bathroom, stared in the mirror, and cried until I had no more tears to cry.

Shaking with dry heaves, I thought: "It didn't work. I gave it all I had, and it didn't work. All those mornings I got up at 4:00 A.M. to study don't even matter. All those recommendations in my placement file mean absolutely nothing. He doesn't give a damn about my ability. All he sees is the wheelchair." And slowly I realized that my best had not been good enough.

As I saw with crystal clarity the injustice of life,

my tears turned to frustration and rage. Searching for a way to vent the feelings of helplessness surging through me, I picked up a large, white Fuller Brush comb and broke it in half, a feat which would have been physically impossible without the flow of adrenalin which was pouring through my body. With the snap of the comb, my mind was off and racing.

Snapping Back

"Doesn't he realize he already has crippled people on his faculty?" I angrily challenged. "Doesn't he see that lots of the teachers on his staff have handicaps? The big difference between theirs and mine is that I can't hide mine during an interview, and they can. Just because a handicap isn't visible at first glance is no proof it doesn't exist.

"How about the teacher who is insecure and, as a result, constantly criticizes and demeans his students in order to build up his own ego? How about the teacher who is so disorganized that her chaotic lessons leave the students without clear goals or objectives? Or what about the one who doesn't know his subject matter and fakes it by filling class time with frivolous substitutes?

"Lots of teachers are 'crippled,' but they get hired because their handicaps don't show," Looking at the reflection in the mirror I sighed. "I can't hide this stupid wheelchair. Oh, life isn't fair. Life isn't fair."

Life, of course, isn't fair. But no one ever promised it would be.

Nowhere but Up

I still consider that night to be one of the lowest points in my life. Nothing can ever erase the helplessness I experienced as I saw that I was caught in a trap with no way out. I had absolutely no reason to go on living. Although I did not know it, this was not to be the only time in my life when suicide would come and sit temptingly on my shoulder. However, this night of personal hell would leave me with a strength that had not been there before. And this strength would help me face the other personal and professional losses that were to come later, other times like this one when dying seemed preferable to living.

That same summer, Ball State University offered me an instructorship, and the painful rejection I'd been given by the public schools made possible my entry into the university system. After a summer of joblessness, I was back in the academic world. Because Ball State has a three-year limit on instructorships, I realized that the job would be temporary. Still, I was delighted for the temporary reprieve.

The following three years were everything I'd ever hoped for. During that time I proved to myself, and to those around me, that teaching is a meeting of the minds, and being in a wheelchair doesn't hinder the process. I found that teaching brought forth the best in me, filling every fiber of my being with purpose and meaning. The students and I got along famously. As I gave them my best, they inevitably gave me back theirs. By the end of the three years, I knew beyond a shadow of a doubt that teaching and I were meant for each other.

Strike Two

As my third year came to an end, I started looking for ways to continue teaching. Since I was not yet emotionally or physically ready to leave home, I decided that I would have two options open to me: I'd get a job in the public schools near my parents' home, or I'd start work on my doctorate. As it turned out, neither was possible.

No one in either the city or the county schools wanted to hire me, and Ball State rejected my application for the doctoral program because I had taught only at the university and had no public school teaching experience. I was trapped in my own catch-22. The public schools wouldn't hire me, and I couldn't start work on my doctorate until I had taught in the public schools. Once again I spent an entire summer knowing I'd have no job when September rolled around. But, thanks to an unexpectedly high enrollment as a result of the baby boom, I did.

A few weeks before Fall Quarter began, I was offered a part-time teaching job for just one quarter. Excitedly I accepted their offer to teach afternoon classes at 3:00 and 4:00, hours no tenured teacher would touch. That part-time job for Fall Quarter turned into a full-time job for Winter Quarter, and during Spring Quarter, Ball State changed their requirement on the doctorate, allowing experience in college teaching to be used in place of experience in the public schools. Things fell into place as they offered me a doctoral fellowship so I could start my degree the following year.

Strike Three Doesn't Always Mean You're Out

The next six years of my life were spent teaching, taking classes, and looking toward my future. Knowing that I was now ready to leave home, I started planning what was to be the biggest step in my life. In August, 1970, a year before receiving my degree, I told a friend: "I don't know where I'll be teaching in September, 1971. I am sending applications to over 150 colleges throughout the Midwest. I'm sure some English chairman in some college somewhere will hire me, not because I'm handicapped, but in spite of it. He'll hire me because I'm a darn good teacher." But no one did.

From those one-hundred-fifty applications, I received only one interview, and no job offer. For the third time in my life I was jobless. Only my belief that I'd found my place in life's pattern gave me the courage to keep pounding on closed doors.

Miraculously, the following year when I repeated the process, I had interviews at five universities and received that elusive job offer for which I'd worked so long.

Believe in Your Own Uniqueness

◆ Walking through loss back to wholeness is a perilous trip.

◆ Loss makes us question the logic of life. At this time more than any other we need to reaffirm our religious beliefs and get in touch with our spiritual core. Doing so will remind us that loss has neither erased our uniqueness nor lessened our value.

◆ In our spiritual core, we will find the foundation for all our other internal resources.

DISCOVERING THAT SUCCESS IS INTANGIBLE

"The moral flabbiness born of the exclusive worship of the bitch-goddess Success. That —with the squalid cash interpretation of the word success —is our national disease."

William James,
Letter to H.G. Wells.

L oss juggles our value system, giving our vision a clarity it didn't previously possess. If we allow ourselves to be tuned in to all the nuances of change occurring in our life, we'll discover our priorities and our perspectives have been rearranged.

Perhaps one of the biggest discoveries we make after loss is that things we once took for granted have now acquired significant value, and much of life that society considers valuable seems inconsequential.

What Do You Value?

Fill in the blank with a 3, 2, or 1, using the following scale:
 (3) Very True   (2) Somewhat True   (1) Not True

____ 1. I have many kitchen appliances I've used in the past, found unnecessary and unneeded, and stored in the back of a cabinet or in the basement.

____ 2. I'm one of the first to own the latest technological toy. I own at least five of the following items: a stereo system, a VCR, a CD player, a Walkman, an answering machine, a mobile telephone, a computer, a camcorder, a portable TV.

____ 3. Current clothing styles are important to me. I buy the latest fashions, knowing they will be dated and unused in three or four years.

____ 4. When paying bills each month, I seldom pay the figure in the balance due column, sending instead an installment payment.

____ 5. I'd rather have a million dollars than good health; with that much money I could buy medical care if needed.

—— 6. It's important that my children have clothes, toys, and possessions similar to those of their peers.

—— 7. I spend more hours a day talking to my colleagues at work than I spend talking to my children.

—— 8. I spend more hours a day watching television than I spend in conversation with my spouse.

—— 9. I've put off many activities I'd like to do such as gardening, reading, playing the piano, learning French, or taking walks because I'm just too busy.

—— 10. My spouse and I both are working and bringing home two paychecks so we can give our children a better life.

If your score is 15 or more, you may value tangible things more than intangible.

REALIZING THE VALUE OF SIMPLE THINGS

All of us have heard the cliché, "A person never appreciates something until it's gone." Like most clichés, this one is grounded in truth. Whether we've lost a person, a job, or our health, with that loss comes a keener appreciation of what has been taken away.

When we daily experience a person's love, we come to accept it, even expect it. When living in the same house with someone, we seldom are consciously aware of how nice it is to share a meal, a hug, or a sunset, but when that person leaves us and the house echoes with emptiness, we realize the value of that which is no longer a part of our life.

Likewise, when we have a steady job calling us out of bed each morning, we often consider it an unwanted eight-hour interruption in our day. But when we are jobless for months on end, when life stretches ahead of us, a meaningless series of days without purpose, we then see the value of what we've lost.

This same attitude prevails when we are healthy and free of pain. Only after a bout with illness, only after some part of our under-appreciated body has lost its ability to silently serve us, do we become aware of how beautifully a healthy body functions, how wonderful it is to be free of pain. Only then do we perceive how great it is to feel normal.

And there we have the magic word: normal.

THE JOY
OF A NORMAL DAY

While going through loss, we discover something which most of the world overlooks—the value of a normal day. Always before, these days of routine living have passed us by as uneventful, twenty-four-hour periods. Suddenly we learn to treasure these normal days filled with marvelous moments free of sorrow, loneliness, or pain. We begin to see a normal day in a totally new light, and we yearn for its return.

During one of the many losses which life has handed me, I turned to John Powell's *Fully Human Fully Alive* for support. I was startled to see my exact feelings reflected from the printed page: "Normal Day, let me be aware of the treasure you are."

Feeling a kinship with Mary Jean Iron who wrote the meditation, I responded in the margin of my book, "Yes! Oh, Yes!" In the nine years since I first read those words, I have realized repeatedly that nothing deepens our appreciation of a normal day like a walk through loss.

THE VALUE OF EVERYDAY THINGS

This desire for a normal day prompted Brenda, a forty-four-year-old woman recently separated from her husband, to come to my home one frosty February evening. Calling first to be sure I could see her, she announced, "I'm at the end of my rope. I've simply got to get out of this empty house. Can I come over and talk?" The call was not a surprise. Brenda had kept in touch since being my student two years previously, and I knew she was having a hard time dealing with the loss of her husband.

"I really had no idea how much I'd miss the daily routine of life with Rob. Every moment in that house is a reminder of him, and it seemed like today it was just one thing on top of another," she explained after curling up on one end of my couch. "When I woke up this morning and saw that empty pillow on the bed beside me, I thought of all the mornings I'd leaned over to kiss awake the face that was no longer there. Shaking off the memory, I walked out in the kitchen, took two cereal bowls and two spoons from the cupboard, and didn't even realize what I'd done until I set them on the table. Can you believe it! He's been gone now for over six months, and I still got out two bowls, rather than one."

She glanced over at me, watching for my reaction. "Yes, I can believe it," I assured her. "Those little habits make you aware how much your life has changed."

Brenda continued, "Things like that are so depressing that I just want to go back to bed and forget the world. But I put away the dumb extra bowl and sat down to eat breakfast. I looked out the window and saw that last night's snow had left a soft blanket of white all over the yard. I watched as four cardinals darted from limb to limb, looking like red balls within the green and white of the spruce trees. It was plain beautiful, and I ached to show it to Rob. As I poked around at my Raisin Bran, I kept thinking that beauty is meant to be shared and the one person I want most to share it with doesn't want to be a part of my life."

She paused again to be sure I was understanding her frustration, her longing for normalcy. Sensing that I was, she said, "Somehow I pushed my thoughts down inside me, finished breakfast, and headed for classes. In history I got back that test we took last Friday, and would you believe I got a 96 on it! When she handed me the paper, I was elated! But as I was driving home, the joy lessened and depression set in again. Getting a high grade is no fun when I can't share the excitement with Rob. I know how silly it sounds, but when I got home I unlocked the front door, walked into that empty house, and said softly, 'Rob, I'm home. I got a 96 on my history test.' When I realized what I'd done, I just sat down and cried.

"These six months have shown me the value of all the little everyday incidents that I used to take for granted. I'd like nothing more than to turn back the calendar to a year ago and live a common, normal day again. Believe me, if I could do that, I'd look at life a lot differently than I did then."

You Can't Go Back, But You Can Use What You've Learned

Many of us have wished for a chance to turn back the hands of time, but few are fortunate enough to get second chances. The lucky ones who do often discover that they have gained a new perspective on life. As it turned out, Brenda was one of these fortunate few. After being divorced for over three years, she and Rob remarried and started a new life together, a life which is stronger now because of the changing values that loss brought into their lives while they were separated.

I also was given a second chance.

THE TOTAL SCHEME OF THINGS

During those six sterile, empty years after the wreck when I had absolutely no hopes and no future, for all practical purposes I was dead. Because of that, I now look on every normal day as my second chance at life. This attitude throws rainbows over days that other people would consider commonplace.

Even on those mornings when the alarm rings and I'm too tired to get out of bed, I thank God that I have a job to get me moving. This appreciation helps put every aspect of my professional life into perspective. While other professors are complaining about all the unpleasant inconveniences of their job, I seldom find within myself grounds for serious dissatisfaction. Even in the midst of all the normal problems of any day (and every job has them), I'm always aware that the problems are insignificant compared to the fact that I have a job.

Something as commonplace as my body's ability to function smoothly, to do what I want it to do, now gives special meaning to a normal day. Going for months without the ability to dress myself, wash my hair, cook my meals, or care for my house, I now have a changed attitude toward these simple skills. Being able to do them again makes any day special.

Having someone we love, a job we enjoy, and a body that works are daily occurrences for most of us. Yet, nearly all of us take them for granted—until that awful day when they are taken away.

A NEW SET OF VALUES

But as loss takes away, I've found it also gives us one of our strongest internal resources: a new set of values.

Loss teaches us that we're terribly vulnerable, that at any moment the script we've carefully written for our life can be edited or deleted. It brings us a keener awareness of our mortality, of our need to wring meaning out of every moment of the life we have left.

Suddenly time is more precious to us than it has ever been before.

As loss is juggling our values, we find we need a mental yardstick for measuring the worth of activities. After walking through a loss, many of us for the first time in our lives find the things we really want to do. Before loss, we say, "I haven't had time to call the neighbor, read the book, play the piano, write the thank-you note, visit the relative, answer the letter." In reality that's not true. Loss can teach us that we all have time to do almost *anything* we want to do. What we don't have is time to do *everything* we want to do.

The Choice Is Ours

Saying "Yes" to one thing means saying "No" to something else. We choose what we *are* going to do, and the very act of choosing defines what we're *not* going to do. Life, we discover, is a series of trade-offs. A generation which has made a mantra of "You can have it all" finds this hard to grasp.

While deciding which things to say "Yes" to, we see clearly that we have a limited amount of time, energy, and money. It's going to be impossible to have every-thing, do everything, and be everything that the world says we should. So what are we going to have, do, and be? The question looms large after we've suf-fered a loss.

KNOWING WHAT'S IMPORTANT GIVES LIFE FOCUS

We start asking ourselves, "What's important in life? What makes a person successful?" We know if we can find the answers to those questions, we'll then be able to use our time, energy, and money on only those things. And so we start searching for what John Powell in *Unconditional Love* (Tabor Publishing, 1978) calls a "life principle."

He urges us to ask ourselves, "What do we *really* want out of life? What do we *really* think will make us happy?" He continues, "You and I are now practicing a life principle, which may not be obvious from a surface view. Someday it will amount to a life wager. In the end everyone gambles his or her life on something, or someone, as the way to happiness."

Is the Choice Worth the Risk?

After dealing with a loss, each of us begins wondering which things in life are worth the gamble.

Answering this question is difficult because society has four common myths about success.

Myth 1: SUCCESS IS HAVING LOTS OF MONEY

Ask any college freshman what makes a person successful, and nine times out of ten the answer will be,

93

"Money—lots and lots of money." Ask any college freshman what will bring her happiness, and invariably the answer will be "All the things that money can buy." To these students the road to success will have no bumps or potholes if only they can devise a way to acquire everything their parents own, plus everything their parents want but can't afford.

It would be nice to think that these replies which my students give yearly are not an accurate reflection of society in general, but logic tells us differently. Where did they get these beliefs? From us, that's where. Parents, peers, teachers, television, magazines, and movies all bombard them with the belief that success is measured by the amount of money people have and the possessions that money will buy.

Myth 2: SUCCESS IS A MEASURABLE COMMODITY: MORE IS BETTER

The more we acquire, goes the logic, the more successful we are. We've all fallen into the numbers trap: "How much money does he make? How many cars, campers, and boats does he own? How much did she pay for her house? How many decks, skylights, and bathrooms does it have? How many degrees has he received? How many articles has he published? How many sales has she made? How much was her commission?" Society views success as a measurable commodity.

How much and *how many* have become the American way of life. Numbers tell the story. Can it be counted? Can it be measured? Does he have lots of it? Then society pronounces him successful.

Myth 3: MONEY WILL SATISFY OUR WANTS AND OUR NEEDS

This generation is not the first to be preoccupied with money and what it will buy. For years Americans have been hopelessly caught up in the pursuit of possessions and have spent amazing amounts of time and energy acquiring them. Obviously, some of this pursuit is necessary, even desirable. Clearly money, in and of itself, isn't bad. Our expectations, however, of what it can do are another story.

Obviously, money can get us food, clothing, shelter, and medical care, things that are necessary for our physical well being and which we cannot do without. We all know that we must care for our bodily needs, and yet how easily we all trip over the difference between wants and needs.

We need food, but we don't *need* frozen dinners, prepared mixes, pretzels, and soda. We need clothes, but we don't *need* Evan Picone suits, London Fog coats, or Guess jeans. We need shelter, but we don't *need* a house with a mortgage which swallows forty percent of our monthly income.

Myth 4: MONEY WILL BRING JOY AND SATISFACTION

Another thing that money can do is buy pleasure and fun, necessary diversions in the midst of life's seriousness. But too often we confuse pleasure and fun with joy and satisfaction, qualities money cannot buy.

When our life is filled with frustration and we're feeling less than successful, we often go on spending sprees, hoping our purchases will bring pleasure back into a joyless life. Rather, we discover within us no lasting joy, no inner satisfaction, but an insatiable thirst leading us into a spiral of purchase after purchase. Pleasure and fun, we find, are fleeting.

As the fascination wears off one new toy, we discard it for a newer, brighter replacement. We discover that the VCR, the compact disc player, and the video camera soon have to be replaced by an updated, more expensive model. We find that the car we polished lovingly four years ago now looks old beside the newer models, and we start shopping for a more stylish replacement. Erich Fromm sees this vicious cycle clearly in *To Have or To Be?* when he reminds us that once something is purchased, it "requires one to consume even more, because previous consumption soon loses its satisfactory character." Indeed, money and all it can buy will not give us lasting joy nor satisfaction.

And although society screams the opposite, money does not make us successful.

Over one hundred and eighty years ago, Wordsworth wrote,

> *"The world is too much with us; late and soon,*
> *Getting and spending, we lay waste our powers:"*

The words have echoed through the years and now come home to rest. We of the late twentieth century have been programmed so well to believe that success comes from "getting and spending" that we constantly buy into this false belief. And in the process we "lay waste our powers."

YOU CAN'T BUY REAL SECURITY

If we don't feel successful, if we feel like we're only chasing rainbows, we decide that material possessions will fill the void within us. Although others may pronounce us successful, we know differently. Even when the rich and famous, possessing everything money can buy, commit suicide, we blindly pursue the myth that success is tangible.

After walking through a significant loss, we often see the fallacy of the myth.

SUCCESS AS MEASURED BY SOCIETY WON'T GET US THROUGH A CRISIS

While all around us people are measuring success by the number of boats and bathrooms a person has, we discover the things which give life meaning cannot be bought, saved, or sold. We become aware that the tangible possessions that were once so important in our lives have now lost their lustre, and material things we coveted offer no comfort in the face of grief and rejection.

When life crashes down around us, when loss is overwhelming, we begin to question society's definition of success. When our world shatters, we discover that neither money, fame, power, nor prestige can put our world back together again. Only our own internal resources will keep us afloat and bring us through the storm.

Walking through this storm makes us look at success as we've never looked at it before. Often for the first time in our lives we see that the seeds for a successful life are within us: our choices, our attitudes, and our priorities make us who we are.

WHO WE ARE IS FAR MORE IMPORTANT THAN WHAT WE HAVE

This distinction between who we are and what we have is made by Erich Fromm when he tells us that the world consists of "having" people and "being" people, and most of us are a complex combination of both. As having people we desire to own, to possess, and to control objects around us, while as being people we are content with "inner activity, the productive use of our human powers."

Success is coming to terms with these paradoxes within us, until the being person dominates the having one. Fromm believes that only to the extent that we decrease the having—stop finding security and identity by clinging to what we have—can we increase the being. This is a hard step to make. After loss, however, this step becomes easier as we see the limitations of our tangible possessions.

WHAT SUCCESS REALLY IS

After we see that success is internal and intangible, after we quit seeking it in possessions and prestige, we move from being fragmented to being focused. We now have an answer to the questions, "What's important in life? What makes a person successful?" We now have that needed mental yardstick for measuring the worth of our activities and possessions.

Realizing that anything which strengthens our internal resources is valuable, we start seeking out those things. Through trial and error we discover ways to cultivate our inner activity.

The roads which people take toward the cultivation of their internal resources are as varied as the individuals who take them. Each of us will choose slightly different paths, leading to slightly different choices, attitudes, and priorities.

I've discovered I gain inner strength from nature, books, and friends, that a healthy body is more important than a high income, and that giving love is more satisfying than gaining possessions. Knowing that who I am is more important than what I have gives me my own personal yardstick of relative value and helps me decide how to spend my time, energy, and money. Give me a free day and I'll spend it reading, writing, and thinking. Give me a hundred dollars, and I'll buy books, daffodil bulbs, and bird seed. Give me a thousand dollars and I'll save it to pay for the best medical care available when I'm ill, or spend it on some delicate river birches to dance in the backyard sunlight when I'm well. My mental yardstick helps me make choices and set priorities.

After we move from fragmented to focused, we find it easier to measure the worth of the activities in our own life. Before giving an activity our time and energy, we can test it against a yardstick of four questions.

Testing Your Values

◆ Am I doing it to make my internal self stronger, or am I doing it because someone, or society, thinks I should?

◆ Is it something which will help me become the type of person I am trying to become?

◆ Is it going to permanently improve me, or serve only as an additional line in my resume?

◆ Is it going to refresh and rejuvenate, or only temporarily distract?

We find it easier to measure the degree of success in our lives when we know what questions to ask.

Test Your Own Success Rating

To how many of the following questions can you give a positive, resounding, "Yes"?

◆ Am I a loving, kind, caring individual?

◆ Am I filled with inner peace, serenity, and stability?

◆   Am I positive, joyful, and content?

◆   Do I like the person I am becoming?

◆   Do I welcome each day?

◆   Do I laugh easily?

◆   Do I enjoy my friends and my family?

◆   Do I have a good relationship with God?

◆   Do I have something to hope for, a goal I'm working toward?

◆   Do I have someone to love?

If you can answer, "Yes," to these questions, you know you are walking in the right direction. Once you have given your life this focus, you have made an important step toward wholeness.

A focused life helps us see that success isn't something we acquire at the end of a journey; rather, it's how we respond to the journey itself. Success doesn't come from money, prestige, or degrees; it's a process, not a product. It's not where we are or what we've got. It's how we felt about ourselves and others as we were getting there.

What's important in life? Anything that enriches our internal resources. Who's successful? Anyone who has cultivated these resources and is living a meaningful life—in spite of loss.

6

LISTENING
WITH LOVE

*"The worst days of darkness
through which I have ever
passed have been greatly
alleviated by throwing myself
with all my energy into some
work relating to others."*
President James A. Garfield

When going through loss, it is normal to become
self-centered and me-focused. Although none
of us likes himself very well while he's the center of
his own little universe, we find it difficult to break
free of the self-pity that's wrapped itself around our
lives.

After the wreck I remember feeling that if I didn't find
some way to get outside the chains of self-pity, I'd be
forever mired in meaninglessness. At that time I was
convinced I was a hopeless case. As all my losses came
tumbling towards me, I found my whole world was
myself. For years I struggled to move away from the

"Barbara-centered" (poor me; all my dreams washed down the drain) person I had become, but I made very little progress. I'd tell myself that I must fight this self-centeredness, but I didn't fight it.

Then I discovered a way out: Love is the answer.

SELF-LOVE IS HEALTHY; SELF-CENTEREDNESS IS DEADLY

Lately love has gotten a lot of bad press. The word is misused and abused, stretched to cover everything from erotic desire to fondness for hot fudge sundaes. We live in a society where the chemical call of the hormones is interpreted as falling in love, where loving oneself is more important than loving others. As stated in chapter four, self-love is a necessary foundation for all our other internal resources, but when self-love becomes self-centeredness, it becomes self-serving.

If my college freshmen haven't fallen into the trap of believing that love is synonymous with sex, they have fallen prey to the current philosophy that love consists of winning by intimidation. When I have them respond to the essay "What's Wrong With 'Me, Me, Me?,'" I'm quickly told, "Nothing!" To the majority of these students, love is climbing in bed with their current partner and/or assertively demanding their own rights. Love is difficult to find in a society obsessed with sex and with looking out for number one.

But sex and assertiveness, although important components, fall short of adequately defining this maligned verb.

LOVE IS SOMETHING WE GIVE, NOT SOMETHING WE GET

After a great deal of foundering, hurting, and hunting, I slowly discovered the truth in Eugene Kennedy's statement that life has meaning when we "reach steadily out to others in love."

I like his use of the words "reach steadily out" because they help define the love that heals our torn lives. "Reaching out" implies a giving love, not a taking one. "Steadily" implies loving when it would be easier not to do so. Kennedy is urging us to make our love broader than sex and self-love. He's leading us to what John Powell calls unconditional love, love which is defined as "concern for the satisfaction, security, and development of the one loved." Reaching steadily out to others involves us in what Scott Peck calls "the will to extend one's self for the purpose of nurturing one's own or another's spiritual growth."

These men have captured the elements of love that

distinguish it from the erotic or the egoistic. The love they are defining centers our life outside ourselves—outside our pain, our pity, and our loss. It urges us to get all tangled up in other people's joys, sorrows, fears, and frustrations, to think of love as something we give, not something we get.

One way we can move out of the "me-centeredness" of loss is by losing ourselves in the needs of those around us.

My Self-Centeredness Diminished as I Reached Out to Others

After the wreck, I felt cheated. Quite honestly, I still do. Even so, I realized feeling cheated was one thing, but wallowing in self-pity was a different matter. When my emotions stepped over the line into pitying myself, I found my whole world was "me." Then one day I said to myself, "Okay, Barbara. You probably won't marry. You won't have children. You can't walk and you wet the bed. It isn't fair. It isn't just. But it's a fact. Now what are you going to do about it? What are you going to do to cope with this self-pity and make life meaningful for yourself and for those around you?"

I finally found the answer in the biblical paradox, "He who loses his life for my sake will find it." Francis of Assisi saw the need to get outside our self-centeredness when he wrote, "It is in forgetting ourselves that we find ourselves."

Clearly, love was the answer. But it wasn't going to be sex or self-love to the exclusion of others. Rather I needed to love something or someone enough to get outside myself. How was I going to accomplish this? How could I best give myself to others? How could I practice unconditional love?

Finding the Answers

When I started teaching English over twenty-five years ago, I was ill-prepared for the situation. Although I had a good background in the subject matter, could prepare lesson plans as well as any tenured professor, and had been given a firm foundation in teaching skills, I was uncomfortable with the student-teacher relationship.

As a beginning teacher, I walked a balance beam trying to live with the ambivalent feelings within me. My training had taught me that there was to be an invisible shield, an impenetrable barrier, kept at all times between the teacher and the student. My gut told me that these students needed more of me than the shell they saw behind the desk each day.

I probably wouldn't have sensed this need if I hadn't been an English teacher. We English teachers, more than most teachers, get to know our students' inner thoughts, attitudes, opinions. Since literature is a reflection of life, it can't be discussed and written about without facing some universal truths. Some classes teach students how to make a living, while others teach students how to live. English is one of the latter.

Beyond Who, What, Where, and When

Although a great deal of life is lived on the surface level answering the Where, When, and Who questions (Where do you live?-Work?-Play tennis? When did you graduate?-Get your job?-Move to town? Who is your physician?-Boss?-Dentist?), English plunges us deeper than the surface. Any methods class worth its salt teaches the future teacher that it's the "Why?" and "How?" questions which are going to unlock students' minds and mouths. My students are required to converse with me constantly, either verbally or on paper. In discussions and individual essays they pour out their reactions to the literature they have just read. While answering my "Why" and "How" questions, they give me a glimpse of themselves that teachers in few other disciplines see.

Teaching English made me stop seeing the students sitting in front of me as bodies with names attached and start seeing them for what they really were: individuals carrying an enormous load of fears, frustrations, and problems. As I realized that I had souls and not just names sitting in front of me, I found myself trusting my gut and giving them more of myself.

My first movement toward reaching out was made in the comments I would write at the bottom of essays. During my third year of teaching, a student wrote an essay telling of the emotional scars she had received while living all her life with a mentally ill mother. The comments I wrote back to her were the beginning of a friendship which is still strong. I discovered that this unique communication brought unexpected dividends. After reading my comments at the bottom of their essays, students would often come in for conferences. These talks usually resulted in a better understanding between us for the remainder of the school year. It also produced several delightful friendships when we were no longer student/teacher. Classroom discussions often had the same result. A lesson would sometimes bring a student to my office because our topic had touched an exposed nerve, and he needed to share the pain.

LISTENING IS LOVING

I had found something the world was craving and that anybody could attain: the ability and time to listen. Realizing that one of the best ways to express love for those around me was to listen to them, I started practicing a skill that was to become the center of my life.

The need was, and still is, obvious. The world is crying for someone to listen, but most of us are too busy "running" to respond. People usually talk more than they listen. Even when they quit talking and act like they're listening, they seldom are. "Listen to all the conversations of our world," says Paul Tournier. "They are for the most part dialogues of the deaf." I've found that in a society which talks instead of listens, and listens but doesn't hear, listening with love is in great demand.

I also discovered that along with this capacity to listen comes a second truth: listening isn't easy.

SIX WAYS TO BE AN EFFECTIVE LISTENER

1. Give the speaker your total attention.

2. Stay tuned in for the unspoken feelings behind the spoken words.

3. Look at life from the speaker's point of view.

4. Avoid giving answers and solutions.

5. Go behind external appearances to find the hidden person.

6. Take the risk of sharing someone's pain.

Doing this type of listening requires us to put the

speaker's needs before our own. This is a monumental task. I have failed at it more times than I want to admit. Yet, every attempt has left me richer.

Giving the Speaker Your Total Attention

Although listening demands our total attention, few of us give it. Most of us fill our lives with so many activities that we're always in a hurry to get something finished or somewhere on time. Because of our fast-paced life, we often make people who want to talk with us feel that they're imposing, taking time away from something we'd rather be doing. Usually this is not stated explicitly, but the message comes across loud and clear.

I've been guilty of this. When I'd be sitting in the office grading essay tests and a student would come in unexpectedly to talk with me, I'd keep my finger on the spot where I'd stopped grading. By doing so, I was implying that my grading was more important than what he was saying. Although I'd said nothing to discourage good communication, my actions had done it for me. Usually students are hesitant to talk to a professor under any circumstances, and I was making it even harder by sending mixed signals to my class. "Feel free to stop in the office any time you need to talk," I'd tell them, but when they got up courage to drop by, I'd give them less than my full attention.

As I tried to put myself in their place, I started changing my actions. Turning from the paper before me, laying my red pen down, and looking the student straight in the eye, I try to assure him that I am listening, I care about him, and at that moment he is more important than anything else in that office. At times I have found these actions difficult, taking a great deal of effort, but I have discovered they bring rewards.

The Unspoken Feelings Behind the Spoken Words

Giving someone our full attention helps us learn to listen between the lines, beyond the spoken words to the unspoken feelings which are often more important than what is being said aloud.

We all ask people, "How are you? How's life? How are things going?" Many situations call for no more than the automatic answers "Fine" or "Okay" which unthinkingly come out of our mouths the second we hear the question. But in some settings the answers to these questions can serve as springboards to a meaningful conversation. But the springboard lies more in what's unsaid than in what's said.

When a person replies "Pretty good," he usually means "It's not good, but I'll pretend it is." If we pick up on that telling word "pretty," we can often get the person to explain why his life is "pretty good" and not "great." If the setting is right and he knows we care, he usually tells us. If a person replies, "Oh, I'm hanging in there," he usually means "I've got a problem, but I'm functioning in spite of it." So once again we need to search for why he's hanging on, what problem is pounding his life. By listening between the lines, we often can pry open the door to genuine communication.

Verbs Which Reveal Inner Turmoil

Patti had been living with her boyfriend for six turbulent months. After giving abundant proof that she and the man were looking at life from totally different points of view, she announced that they were nevertheless going to continue their present living arrangement.

"Then you feel the arguments are over and you've settled the big differences," I stated.

"Well, I can handle it," she replied. "I'm going to be able to cope. If things stay the way they are now, I can manage."

I listened to her responses and said, "Patti, your verbs are giving you away. Listen to what you just said: *handle, cope, manage.* They're telling me that this relationship is a burden, but you're going to live with it

113

anyway. Why?" By listening between the lines, I could question her motives and maybe open the door for some genuine answers.

When people talk, they often have hidden agendas of what they'd like to tell us if they could only get a chance. We need to be aware that what the person puts into words is frequently NOT what he really wants to express. By staying tuned in to the slightest suggestion that there is an undercurrent to the words that are coming from his mouth, we can sometimes get that undercurrent to surface.

Hidden Agendas

The student who comes in to discuss a grade, for example, may very well be wanting to talk about something else. "I was really happy to get that 85 on the essay" stated Craig, a bright, energetic student. "But Dad says I'm not working hard enough in here or I'd be getting 95. Of course, I never do anything that pleases Dad."

Picking up on the parenthetical last sentence, I replied, "You feel depressed that your Dad doesn't appreciate how hard you're working in English." With this opening, he told me about the struggle that had been going on for years between him and his parents, the stress that came from feeling he would never be "good enough" to get his Dad's approval, and the mountains of criticism that were shredding his self-confidence, making him wonder if college were really for him. During the conference, I learned things about Craig which helped us both during the remainder of the school year.

Not Enough Time

Giving total attention, however, is not always possible. Somehow students seem instinctively to choose those times for a talk when I'm almost late to class, flying down the hall with my lap full of books and papers. Believing I should be available if a student needs me, I used to attempt balancing talking to the student and rushing toward class. By doing so, I was giving the student less than my full attention, filling myself with guilt for being both a poor listener and a late teacher, and helping no one. Since I can't be two places at once, I now try to tell the student that I'd really like to listen, but at that moment I can't. When possible, I set up a future meeting—either in my office, at home, or on the phone.

To give someone our total attention, we must part willingly with huge hunks of our time. But for most of us, time is in short supply. In a world filled with cooking dinner every night, making beds every morning, scrubbing the toilet every week, paying utility bills every month, changing the car's oil every three months, endlessly pulling weeds in the flower beds, sewing buttons on shirts, and waiting in grocery lines, there seems to be no time left to listen.

Making Listening a High Priority

I have a neighbor, however, who manages to do all the things the rest of us do and still finds time to be a good listener. Whenever my life crashes down, she immediately gives me her undivided attention. When my niece committed suicide, it was JoAn who dropped everything and was at my side in thirty minutes. Although she has a husband and three children, I never felt for a second that I was imposing on her evening.

She brought supper, sat on the couch, and listened for hours as I poured out my sorrow and guilt. A few years later as I dealt with the death of my mother, it again was JoAn who tirelessly listened as I verbalized my regrets, my grief, my emptiness. While the rest of the world is busy meeting deadlines and keeping appointments, my neighbor puts first things first. Although her life is as busy as the next person's, she listens as though she had nothing else in the world to do, giving her total attention. That's listening with love.

Looking at Life from the Speaker's Point of View

Another stumbling block to effective listening is our inability to look at life through the eyes of the person who is talking. When teaching point of view, I tell the students it's important to know who's telling the story because that will bias everything that is said and done. The same is true with listening. We all come to any conversation with our preconceived attitudes, and often these attitudes hinder us from hearing what the other person is saying. It's hard to listen open-mindedly and lovingly to someone whose problem goes against the grain of our own life philosophy. Yet, to be an effective listener, this is what we must try to do.

Students often share with me things that they won't tell their parents. I'm no more accepting of alcohol, abortion, drugs, divorce, sleeping around, or extra-marital affairs than their parents; I do, however, try to set aside my preconceived attitudes toward their actions while I'm listening to their problems. A friend once asked me if I wasn't encouraging their negative behavior by listening to their frustrations and fears. The only answer I can give is, "I hope not." My students know where I stand on moral issues. They also know that regardless of where they stand, if they need someone to listen, I'll be there. Unconditional love does not say, "I'll listen if you're behaving as I think you should." The toughest part of unconditional love is saying, "I'll listen. Period."

Avoiding Playing God

Setting our attitudes temporarily aside keeps us from playing God with the speaker's life. How easy it is to give solutions, rather than listen.

Too often I want to comment or give advice before
the other person has said everything he wants to
say. I have to constantly catch myself or I'm saying,
"Oh, I know what you mean. I've gone through exactly the same thing" (or had the same thoughts or
experienced the same emotions). Then I'm anxiously
waiting to tell how I handled the situation when it
was in my life. If I'm not careful, I find myself so
busy planning the witty, wonderful, wise response
I'm going to give, that I'm not really listening. Rather
than concentrating on what's being said, I'm busy
forming a solution to the problem.

This benevolent blundering grew out of my belief
that everyone who came to me needed answers, solutions, advice. This is simply not true. Actually, I was
doing my listeners harm when I let my all-too-human
desire to solve problems get in the way of their need
to express their pain.

In the first place, regardless of what they had
thought, felt, or experienced, the *same* thing did not
happen to me. Because each person is unique, we
could not have identical experiences—similar maybe,
but not the same. Later, much later, in a conversation
or a friendship it may be helpful to let the person
know that we have experienced emotions much like
his, but doing so too quickly does more harm than
good. At many stages, emotional pain has no solution,
and we rob the person of his grief and sorrow when
we attempt to give one. And equally important, the

person doesn't really want to hear how we handled it. Not yet. She simply wants us to hear about the pain that is throbbing through her life. People who are hurting need our ears more than they need our mouths.

I'm convinced that everyone who has ever succeeded in becoming a good listener has had to stifle this tendency to give easy answers and soothing solutions. Failure to stifle it will effectively cut off communication at the roots. It helps to remind ourselves that listening is not done for the purpose of solving problems. Listening is done to encourage and help someone express his thoughts and feelings. Listening may indeed solve problems, but it's the speaker who does the solving, not the listener. Verbalizing his feelings often helps him sort and sift through the tangled emotions that are holding him hostage. The very act of putting his feelings into words is therapeutic as he clarifies his thoughts and finds his own solutions.

Going Behind External Appearances to Find the Inner Person

Effective listening, although difficult to practice, is an integral part of loving, of losing our self-centeredness. If we decide to make love a part of our lives, we need to recognize the fact that it's going to be hard work. There are many times I'm not sure I want to work that hard.

Some students give false images, making it very difficult for me to like them, let alone love them. These
masks become barriers that I must climb over before
I can ever hope to know the person hiding within.
The big question facing me is always, "Do I want to
make the effort?"

Living through the boys' shoulder-length hair of the
'60s, the unisex punk haircuts of the '70s, and
the green-streaked tangled tresses of the '80s, I've
learned that what's outside seldom accurately re-
flects what's inside. More importantly, I've learned
that the student who drives me crazy for the first
three weeks of class may turn out to be a close friend
three years later. Often I am reminded of John Powell's statement: "I swear that everybody I try to reject by classification God sends back into my life to
educate me."

Beyond the Facades

Tim was one of my rejections. Hair flowing over his
shoulders, cigarette constantly in his hand, jeans torn
over each knee, this young man was always late to
class. I'd be halfway through a beginning quiz when
he'd saunter into the classroom, take his seat, and
give me a "Now what are you going to do?" look.
What I wanted to do was throw him out of class. But
as I got acquainted with this "reject," I found a sensi-
tive, hard-working man who was taking twelve hours

of class work, making good grades, and yet working eight hours each night to help his widowed mother support their family. It was impossible for him to arrive on time because he came to class straight from night shift, drove across crowded Cincinnati during the morning rush hour, and then ran up three flights of stairs. Rejection gave way to admiration.

Gary was another one of my rejections. After watching him walk into class the first day, I was sure he'd never make it in college. His bushy beard, long hair, and earring combined to make me question whether he belonged in the class, and whether I could tolerate his being there. His classroom answers were sprinkled with "You're damned right" and "Hell, no." The other students weren't quite sure how to react to him; little did they know that I was totally at a loss myself. But, once again, I had to swallow my first impression as I learned that Gary was an active member of Alcoholics Anonymous, worked in a halfway house for the mentally ill, and wrote some of the most perceptive essays of any of the students in the class.

One of my memorable rejects was Marla. Coming into my class the first day, she gave me that "Just try to teach me something" look that teachers sense in an instant. With a chip on her shoulder, a pout on her mouth, and a frown on her face, she was a constant irritation, a proverbial thorn in my side. I vacillated between treating her kindly and ignoring her coldly. By the middle of the Fall Quarter, I was nearly at my wits' end. I kept asking myself, "How can this girl who acts as if she hates my English class be such a good writer?"

And magically one of her essays unlocked our standoff. She told me on paper about her sister's recent suicide, her deep grief, her haunting guilt. After marking the essay's punctuation, grammar, sentence structure, spelling, organization, and specific support, I put the grade on the top of the first page. Then I turned the essay over and wrote a page-long note—not from an English teacher, but from a friend, responding totally to the grief and guilt she was experiencing. I had discovered the cause for her mask and found behind it a hurt soul. After that essay, her facial expression, her tone of voice, and her attitude toward class reflected that she had shared her unbearable pain.

These and scores of other students remind me once again how much effort it takes to love, how easily we all shrink from making that effort, and how important it is to plunge ahead when we'd rather quit. Each time that God sends a Marla or a Gary back into my life to educate me, I stand in awe of the power of love. I'm always reminded of these lines by Edwin Markham:

> He drew a circle that shut me out—
> Heretic, rebel, a thing to flout.
> But Love and I had the wit to win:
> We drew a circle that took him in.

Life repeatedly reminds me how much time, energy, and patience must go into drawing that circle. Over and over I find I lack that time, energy, and patience. Over and over I find I don't want to make the effort.

A Two-Way Street

Unconditional love asks, however, that we give up some of ourselves to make room for this new person in our life. It calls us to be loving even when we'd rather not, when it's inconvenient. We can't love him only when it fits our schedule. This becomes a tremendous problem when our lives are already full to overflowing.

A Case for Hope

Seventeen years ago when I first met Doris, she was tangled in a web of circumstances, some of her making, others beyond her control. Only a few months before Fall Quarter began, she had given birth to a child whom she had then given up for adoption. In an attempt to get her life headed in a new direction, she was entering college at age thirty. As I got to know her better, it was clear she was the only mature (or sane) member of her family. Her father was abusive and violent, her mother mentally ill, her unmarried sister had given birth to three children, one brother was an alcoholic and involved in hard drugs, and the other brother was totally out of touch with reality, constantly in and out of the state mental hospital. All six of these adults lived under the same roof, each increasing the amount of turmoil in Doris's life. Since graduating from high school, she had worked long hours as a waitress. While pregnant she had decided to use the little money she had saved to go to college and, as she put it, "get a decent job so I can afford to get out of that zoo I'm living in."

I was attracted to Doris by her determination, her bright mind, and her sheer guts. She had decided to use her brains to break away from the maelstrom that was engulfing the rest of her family. When she graduated, got a good job, and finally moved into her own apartment, I was proud of her. I was not prepared, however, for what followed.

For the next six years she called my home at least three times a week. During these hour-plus monologues, I listened to unending streams of self-pity and complaining. As months turned into years, my patience grew thin. It got so I dreaded to hear the phone ring, fearing it would be her. During this time I stood by and listened as she went through two live-in boyfriends, had an abortion, and made three job changes.

Realizing she needed more help than my non-directive listening could give, I encouraged her to start seeing a psychologist. My hopes for her improvement, however, were short-lived. Neither her psychologist nor I were slowing her steady down-hill slide. The phone calls continued. I watched as she moved from the normal signs of insecurity she had shown when I first met her to repeated cycles of hysteria and depression. All new situations were greeted with alarm—and a phone call to me.

Part of me kept saying, "You're making no headway; she's not improving; she's just using you. Why don't you tell her to get out of your life? After all, there is no reason in the world that you have to be the one to constantly prop her up." But another voice would always answer, "If you really love her, you can't just give up."

About the time I'd be having one of these internal dialogues, the phone would ring. Some new crisis would have entered Doris's life. It might be big or it might be small. No matter. It was earth-shattering in her eyes. I remember one night when she called to announce that her car would not start and therefore it would be **IMPOSSIBLE** for her to go to work the next morning. This was followed by the announce-ment that she'd be fired on the spot, never find an-other job, have no money to pay the rent, and be on welfare within a week. She refused my suggestion of taking a cab or bus to work by saying, "A cab will cost $40, and if I take a bus I'll be raped or robbed." When I hung up, I made some phone calls. After pricing a cab and getting bus routes, I eagerly called her back to share the news that a cab cost only a few dollars and the bus stopped at the corner where she worked. Blindly ignoring the facts, she continued to say she could not possibly get to work. The whole ordeal ended when a neighbor came over and started her car for her. In the meantime I had been on the phone for over two hours. Sitting there I wondered if I was doing the right thing to listen with love. What if I was only making her dependent on me? What if I were wasting my time and energy on a hopeless case?

But I kept listening. During the following three years the phone calls lessened. Still, her life was a simmering pot of problems. Living with a new boyfriend, moving to a different part of town, and becoming pregnant again filled her life with enough frustrations that she'd usually panic, call me once or twice a week, and then dig in and cope. I felt better about her until one night nearly nine years after I met her.

For over a month she had been filled with hopelessness, telling me repeatedly she had no interest in life, no desire to get out of bed, no reason to make new friends. The man she had been living with had walked out of her life, leaving her with an empty apartment, unpaid bills, and four months pregnant. Around eight o'clock one night my phone rang. "Just give me one good reason I shouldn't kill myself tonight," challenged Doris. "Oh no," my mind raced. "I'm not up to this. I don't have the lesson plans reviewed for tomorrow, there are still six essays I have to grade before I go to bed, and I have to wash my hair." Horrified, I listened to my mind.

Here was a woman at the end of her string and I was thinking about everything but her. Quickly getting myself together, I listened as she talked, and over two hours later we both felt better. That conversation became a pivotal point in Doris's life. I realized that if I hadn't listened to all the other calls before this one, she might not have reached out to me when she really was going to kill herself.

As she gained self-confidence in the years that followed, the calls became less frequent and more positive; I found that I no longer dreaded her calls. During this time she frequently thanked me for all the years that I'd listened. "You were always there," she said one night. "I can see now that I must have driven you crazy. But you never gave up on me, did you?" "No," I answered, and then thought, "But I'm glad you don't know how often I wanted to."

Yet, wanting to give up—and giving up—are two totally different things. Listening with love is a daily challenge. It's hard work at times, and often inconvenient. No one does it well 100% of the time. I know that there are many days when I do a rotten job. There are nights I go to bed knowing that I've handled life poorly that day. I can know the right thing to say and do, but actually saying and doing it is a whole new ball game. The much-repeated phrase "Love works if you work at it" holds a great deal of truth.

Taking the Risk of Allowing Someone's Pain to Enter Your Life

Love is not only a lot of work; it is also a risk.

While attending a crisis-line class a few years ago, I was having a philosophic conversation with a new friend, Wilma, whose husband had just divorced her and whose father had recently died. Overwhelmed with loss, she was questioning me about the power of listening with love. "But the risks, the pain," she commented. "Any time we love someone we open ourselves up for hurt, for agony. And after we've been hurt a few times, shouldn't we learn to protect ourselves? I mean the risks are tremendous. The person is either going to disappoint us, walk out on us, or die. Do you think it's really worth the risks?" Instinctively I responded, "Oh, yes!" (At times I throw nondirective counseling out the window!)

Retreating

Later as I was leaving the meeting, I realized I'd been a poor listener by answering too quickly. Anything said to her right then wouldn't have mattered. She wasn't ready to listen and would have to discover through the trials and errors of her own life that it was worth the risks. While going through two losses at the same time, she was doing what we all do: protecting herself from future pain. During times of loss we all feel the need to wrap our arms tightly around ourselves for comfort, for security, for protection. We intend never, never, never to reach out to anyone again. We make up our minds that absolutely no one is going to put us in a position to experience this blinding pain again.

Ironically, these are the very times in our life that we most need to focus our attention outside ourselves. I've found that the whole experience of living is a two-edged sword: if we allow ourselves to get all tangled up in other people's lives, we risk having pain in our own lives; but if we refuse to take that risk, we're left with an orderly, empty, sterile world. Each of us decides which side of the sword is the most painful. Those who have lived on both sides of this sword know that intermittent pain is preferable to unending emptiness.

We live in a society where people go to great lengths to avoid any amount of emotional pain. Living in our little cells of isolation, we are conditioned very early to use that isolation as a protection. "Don't get too close," we admonish. "Don't invade my space. Don't get involved." But the more we close ourselves off from others, the more empty and sterile our neat little lives become. By not getting involved, by never taking the risk of love, we avoid pain. We also, however, avoid living.

As the pain of our own loss lessens, we find we want to reach out to those around us. By helping others deal with their sorrow, hurt, and loss, we become more human. As we cultivate our internal resources of listening with love, meaning comes back into our shattered lives. Giving one's self away—one's time, energy, attention—is a difficult, and yet satisfying, step in our healing process. In many ways it is the greatest gift we can give another person—or ourselves.

LIVING LIFE IN
SMALL SLICES

> *"The Present, the Present is*
> *all thou hast*
> *For thy sure possessing;*
> *Like the patriarch's angel*
> *hold it fast*
> *Till it gives its blessing."*
>> John G. Whittier,
>> "My Soul and I," Stanza 34

While going through loss, many of us decide that life is meaningless, and we approach this meaningless present as something to be gotten through, not something to be experienced. Immediately following our loss, this is a healthy attitude. Later, however, the same attitude can easily become a stumbling block, hindering our healing.

Finding no meaning nor satisfaction in the present moment, we glue our eyes and our energy on some distant event or time when we believe our life will magically acquire meaning. If only we can put up with the present, we tell ourselves, life will be beautiful in some far-distant future. Happiness, we assure ourselves, will come *after* we get our degree, our next promotion, a new job, a raise, the mortgage paid, or the kids raised.

THE BEST TIME IS NOW

This focus on the future encourages us to ignore the present. And yet the present is all that is real. The past is gone and the future does not exist. Our entire life consists of present moments—right here, right now, and one of our strongest internal resources results from an awareness of these moments.

Living in the Now requires cultivating a special sensitivity, an acute awareness, to what is going on both inside and outside ourselves each moment of our life. Developing this awareness, we discover we need not wait to reach life's remote landmarks in order to find meaning in life. Meaning, we discover, occurs in unexpected moments while we are working toward those landmarks. We find that the best time is not some wonderful future moment; the best time is Now and all the "Nows" of all our tomorrows.

Living in the Now Is Not Living for the Moment

Because living in the present is a recurring theme in literature, it often becomes the topic of classroom discussion. Listening to my students for over twenty years, I now know the direction of this discussion before the students even open their mouths.

After pinpointing the main ideas in the essay or story, I'll ask, "What does the author mean? How are we going to get the most meaning out of the present moment?" Quickly hands shoot up. "He means that you only go around once, and you should pack in all the experiences that you can," answers one student. Another agrees, "He means eat, drink, and be merry for tomorrow you may die." "Yes," adds a friend. "Go for it. Do all the things you want to do. If something makes you feel good and makes you happy, do it." Another chimes in, "Get drunk and have a ball. Get high and forget your troubles. Party, party, party."

When I first started teaching, I was unprepared for these responses. I can still remember my mental gymnastics as I tried to hide my dismay.

After years of teaching, I now know what to expect and patiently let students express these same ideas—year after year. When all members of the class have had an opportunity to assure me that the author is

133

giving them the green light to raise hell, I write two phrases on the board:

> living **IN** the moment
> living **FOR** the moment

"How does changing the preposition change the meaning of the phrase?" I prod. Nearly always some student sees that living *in* the moment leads to an awakening of our senses and a keener appreciation of life, while living *for* the moment leads to a deadening of our senses and a temporary blotting out of life.

It's Easy to Numb Ourselves with Outer Stimuli

My students, and society in general, fail to make this crucial distinction when deciding what it means to "live each day fully." The pursuit of instant gratification is fast becoming the American way of life. Many people choose this dead-end alley because it's easy. Look around. You'll see people in every walk of life drugging themselves with external stimuli, refusing to rely on their own internal resources. By passively bombarding themselves with these outer stimuli, they miss the chance to live *in* the moment because they are trapped by their attempt to live *for* the moment. As long as we anesthetize ourselves with escapes, we'll do nothing but numb ourselves and make awareness of the present impossible.

Narcotics, hallucinogens, and alcohol all do an effective job of eliminating the Now. They can be used either to create a transient euphoria or to blot out all reality—neither of which enhances our awareness of the present moment.

When we see life through a haze of hallucinogens, the Now becomes a distorted, twisted reality. Drugs don't solve problems; they only mask them. And when the transitory, temporary, mask slips—when the high is over—reality is still there staring us in the face. Drugs force us to live *for* the moment and leave us in even worse shape after we've used them. John Powell in *Unconditional Love* calls this the "cult of experience" and says: "When empty people reach out to eat, drink, and be merry as a program of fulfillment, the hangover is worse than the hunger."

Television is another effective escape. There are millions of people who know more about the characters in television shows they watch than they know about their neighbors. They would rather watch T.V. than carry on a conversation with their families. Sadly, these people universally find their day-to-day life lacking when measured against the drama they see on the screen: their bodies not as beautiful, their spouses not as attentive, their children not as witty. For them the line between real and pretend has nearly been erased. Television has become a quick, easy, and socially acceptable way to escape awareness.

Yet, by avoiding these escapes and taking control of our attitudes toward the present moment, we can find the inner strength to face loss and life.

WE CONTROL OUR ATTITUDES

Although we'd all like to press a button and instantly, miraculously, have a positive attitude toward life, it doesn't work that way. Like any habit, a positive attitude is acquired slowly by repetition, by practice.

We choose how we're going to think and how we're going to act. Yet some of us, attempting to avoid taking responsibility for our own lives, convince ourselves that attitudes are not something within our control. We tell ourselves that some people are innately blessed with a positive attitude, while others are cursed with a negative one. This is utter nonsense.

A positive attitude toward the present moment is something each of us chooses. We aren't born with it; we create it daily.

I've found I have to cut life up into little slices and deal with it a slice at a time: one moment, one hour, one day. If I try to think of being positive for the rest of my life, it's overwhelming; I can't tackle all of life at once. Rather than deal with life in big hunks, I try to concentrate on the slice that is directly in front of me: Now.

We Are Constantly Evolving

Each of us is the sum total of all the choices we have made up to this moment; the choices we make today, and all the todays that follow, will make us who we are a year from now—and ten years from now. Daily you and I are creating the person we are going to become.

Since Now is so important, what are we going to do with it? How are we going to spend the next ten minutes, the next hour?

A teacher knows how significant these questions are. In methods class we are told how important it is to "set" the class at the beginning of each new quarter and again at the start of each day's lesson. The teacher's attitude and actions these first few minutes anchor the atmosphere of the class for the remainder of the hour.

I was fortunate to have two excellent methods teachers who taught me this truth. Because I know its importance, I'm very careful how I "set" a class. No matter what my life is like outside that classroom, no matter what personal problems I may be carrying around that day, once I close the classroom door, my problems stay in the hall. When I start the lesson, I make a point to be pleasant and upbeat. When I first started teaching, doing this was forced. Only with a conscious act of will could I change my attitude. But after twenty years of practicing a positive attitude in the classroom, I've discovered that what was once forced behavior is now natural.

How We Spend Each Morning Affects Our Attitudes All Day

I've found that to live in the Now I need to set myself for life, much as I set a class. I've found that beginnings and endings are significant parts of each day, times in which we create the atmosphere that will determine the quality of the hours in between. I'm convinced that how we spend the first and last half-hours of each day affects the very core of our attitude toward life.

Beginning With a Blank Slate

Because I've found this to be true, before I get out of bed in the morning, I "set" myself. Now there are many mornings I'd just as soon not even get out of bed, let alone get out of bed and be positive, but I've learned that my attitude those first moments of the day sets the tone for what's to follow. Each morning I thank God for a brand-new, fresh, clean day and remind myself that at that moment the day is still a blank slate on which to a large extent I can write whatever I choose to write. Knowing that I certainly can't control many of the events that will occur, I remind myself that I can control how I respond to those events. I think of specific qualities I want the world to see in me that day. I think of people I want to influence or help; I name names and set little miniature goals for myself—not for life, not for the week, but just for that day. And I ask God to help me to make a positive difference in the lives of the people I come in contact with.

So am I promising your day will be great if you start it with a positive frame of mind? Of course not. So am I saying that my day is always great because I set myself with a positive attitude? No, of course not.

Bettering the Odds for a Good Day

On many days, more than I like to admit, I fail to be the person I want to be. I have my share of days filled with frustration, depression, and sadness. But just because there are days I get depressed, frustrated, and sad does not necessarily mean it does no good to set myself each morning. It only means I'm human. Obviously, I can't promise anyone a life filled with great days. I can, however, promise that a day will have a much better chance of being great if we *do* start it with a positive frame of mind than if we *don't*.

Setting Our Attitude Throughout Each Day

After a positive beginning, we need to repeatedly set ourselves for each new slice of life we face during the day. In the process, we end up being aware of the present moment, using it as wisely as we know how, and finding meaning where it previously didn't exist.

Something as simple as a shopping trip to the mall can take on new meaning. Rather than something to be "gotten over with," it now becomes a chance to see how actions follow attitudes. We choose how we will respond to the waitress who serves us lunch, the clerks in the department stores, and the other shoppers we meet during the day.

I have a friend with a knack for turning a shopping trip into an opportunity for awareness. Noticing that the restaurant is unusually crowded, she comments to the harried waitress, "Good grief, you must be exhausted. The restaurant is packed." After listening to a dialogue between a complaining customer and a polite clerk, she tells the frustrated salesperson, "You really handled that well. It takes a lot of patience to deal with some people in this world." Or watching an obviously tired mother shopping with three children in tow, she verbalizes what she's thinking, "I don't see how you do it. Won't you be glad to get them all back home!" In almost every case the person smiles, glad to realize that someone out there recognizes that she's got problems. In almost every case awareness brings to both the listener and the speaker a ray of recognition concerning their shared humanity. Such an awareness enriches the fabric of our life.

How We Spend the End of Each Day Significantly Affects Our Life

After the day is finished and we climb back into bed, once again we face an important little slice of life— the moments before we fall asleep.

Laura, a former student of mine, found her grades in English slipping. When I talked to her about the problem, she told me that she thought part of the problem was a lack of sleep. "I either can't get to sleep when I go to bed, or I go right to sleep and then wake up at 3:00 and stare at the ceiling for an hour. It's really getting to me," she said. Since there was no physical discomfort to cause this, we talked about possible emotional or mental causes.

"What do you do the half-hour before you go to sleep?" I asked. "Usually I watch television," she responded. "What shows?" I continued. "Oh, anything that's on the tube," was her reply. But when we started listing what she actually had watched during the previous week, five of the nights had been spent watching shows filled with disturbing plots of violence and the other two had consisted of the 11:00 news, which with its rapes, wrecks, and robberies isn't exactly lullaby material. I then asked her what she thought about after she turned off the television and settled down to sleep. Her answer was no surprise. "For a while I think about what I've just been watching, and then I usually start to think about the

141

next day. I make lists in my mind of all the things I have to do and how I'm going to get them done in the little bit of free time I have before and after school."

The Mind Set

Laura, like a lot of the rest of us, was giving herself a negative set for the night. As her mind swirled with plots of television and plans of tomorrow, her body reacted. Sleep was out of the question.

I have my father to thank for helping me learn how to set myself at the close of a day. When I was a little girl, he would often ask, "What was the best thing that happened to you today?" I'd sift and sort through the day's experiences trying to find the very best thing to share with him. I'd tell him that the best thing was "Playing euchre with Uncle James and Aunt Ruth" or "Making chocolate cake with Jean," or "Getting to churn the homemade ice cream." I remember that "Picking flowers in the garden with Mother" or "Reading Nancy Drew all afternoon in the backyard" won the prize on many nights.

Concentrating on the Good

By questioning me like this, he encouraged me to concentrate on the good parts of the day and, in the process, forced me to set priorities. This question and

answer period at the end of the day laid the foundation for a ritual that is still an important part of
my life.

Although it isn't always possible, I usually end the
day by reading something that leaves my mind calm
and tranquil. After closing the book and turning out
the light, I thank God for all the good things that
have been a part of that day. I look back on the last
twenty-four hours and remember all the positive,
joyful, and meaningful moments that have been
present. As in the morning, I try to be very specific:
"Thank you that JoAn and I had a good talk. Thank
you that Rebecca and I had fun eating dinner on the
deck this evening. Thank you that the 10:00 class
was a real joy today." Doing this helps me realize
how many good things I've got going for me as it
reaffirms and makes me aware of the positive parts of
each day.

Shaping the Moment

It's much easier to believe that we're molded by the
moment, rather than that the moment is shaped by
us. Because the idea that we have control over the
Now is disturbing to some people, they deny that
their attitude can change anything.

They're wrong. I've had it happen so many times in
my own life that I'm sure it can. But we need to stay
tuned in to our own thoughts.

OUR MENTAL MESSAGES AFFECT THE COLOR OF OUR NOW

We talk to ourselves all the time, so we'd better start listening to what we're saying. The mental messages we send ourselves each day can either dim or enhance our awareness of the Now. These internal dialogues set the tone of our life, and yet they often go unnoticed. Only by listening to what's moving around in our mind can we flip the switch to a more positive channel.

When I started intently listening to what I was bombarding myself with, I heard a stream of negative reinforcement, consisting of "I'm tired," "I feel rotten," or "My arms ache." Undetected, mental messages such as these can do a lot of harm because they have a profound effect on both the way we think and the way we act. It isn't that the messages are untrue. I may, in fact, be tired, feel rotten, and have arms that ache. My inner dialogue, however, is simply reinforcing the situation. If I tell myself something often enough, it will indeed become true. Even though I can't make the tiredness or pain go away by eliminating the mental message, I can certainly intensify it by repeatedly telling myself it's there.

Playing Mind Games

If I'm able to catch one of these as I'm giving it, I can cut it off, but unless I keep constantly tuned in to

144

what messages I'm sending myself, I can't control them. It's similar to the student who writes "He don't understand me." Ten chances out of ten this is the student who SAYS the same sentence, so I encourage him to monitor his mouth and really listen to what he's saying. Once he starts listening for the subject and verb which don't agree, once he hears the "he don't," he'll start correcting his mouth. And once his mouth changes, his pen will follow. Likewise, our actions will follow our attitudes. Correcting our mental messages will change the color of our Now.

Think back over the last few weeks of your life. Picture yourself doing something which you didn't particularly enjoy, but which had to be done. Think how that job might have been made easier if you'd changed your attitude toward it. I'm not talking about a Pollyanna pie-in-the-sky kind of attitude; I'm talking about a realistic, practical way of altering your thinking.

Working through the Negative

For example, while making bread every week, I often get sick and tired of kneading dough, shaping loaves, and picking the sticky stuff off my fingers. But recalling how much more nutritious this whole-wheat bread I am making is than the white substitute sold at the grocery, I find the job easier. And when I concentrate on the fact that with every punch, pat, and pull I'm using up calories (and helping keep my weight down), the job becomes almost pleasant.

The same thing happens when I have a pile of essays to grade. Feeling terribly sorry for myself, I can easily make the job worse by repeating my litany that "only English teachers have to spend four hours every night grading stupid essays" or "I should have majored in something where I could give objective tests."

But on the flip side of the situation, I can make the whole process more pleasant if I remind myself that my grading helps the student who wrote the paper, that every mark I make has the potential to improve her writing. After all, she has to know what she's doing right and what she's doing wrong before she can improve. And this deliberate change in my attitude not only makes the job more meaningful; it also makes me a better grader.

Another place I see the power of mental messages is when I'm shopping and, after rolling myself the length of the mall, find I'm exhausted. My entire day can be saved if I remind myself that this is one of the few opportunities I get for aerobic exercise, and every single roll I make is improving my cardiovascular system. Suddenly my arms feel stronger and the rolling becomes easier.

In each case, the situation has not changed, but my attitude has.

Coping with the Pain of the Past

Living in the Now not only affects our present; it also can lessen the pain of the past as well as the fear of the future.

The past is over. We can't go back. We can't undo the loss. Although we know that part of our life is gone, never to return, we humans are put together in such a way that at any moment we can mentally journey back in time. And how often we do just that. Dreams (both the night and daytime variety) of what might have been slip easily into our minds. Before we know it, we're reliving the past—daydreaming about how wonderful things were before and agonizing about how empty they've been since. But the moment we do this, we're destroying part of Now.

We all have trouble knowing when to turn from the past and walk in the present. Too often we bang our heads mercilessly against a loss we can't change, rather than accept reality and get on with life.

Life Rarely Offers Second Chances

I often see this in the classroom when one of my students gets an F for the quarter grade. After failing the course, he comes to my office or calls on the phone. "Won't you please change the grade?" he asks. "No," I reply. "It's too late for that." "Then can't I do extra work? Can't I take the final over? Can't I have a second chance?" he begs. On and on go the pleas.

This is the student who has not yet learned there are times in life when we don't get second chances. He is discovering, often for the first time, that some situations exist which simply can't be changed.

"Rather than spending hours of time and energy trying to avoid reality, look life straight in the eye and face facts," I tell him. "This quarter is over. Accept that and remember that next quarter is a brand-new start. Go down to the office right now and register for the course again. Find out who your professor is going to be and what textbook he's using. Go buy the book and start studying *now*. Don't dwell on what's over and done. Put your energy into today."

Even though we know we shouldn't live in the past, even though we know we must live in the present, how difficult it is to do.

Reopening Old Wounds

Beth, a twenty-eight-year-old woman in my class, found this to be true. One day while teaching I noticed she was fighting back tears all during the hour. Since she was sitting in the last row, I felt sure no one but me had noticed her struggle, so I made a point to follow her into the hall as she left class. "Can I help?"

I asked. "Oh, not really. I'm very sorry about the crying. I'm sure it was distracting." I assured her that I wasn't upset by the crying, but I was worried about the cause. "I know you're hurting inside," I said.

"Oh, I am," she replied. "It was two years ago today that the divorce was final. I keep trying to tell myself that January 14 is just another day like every other day of the year, but it isn't working. It's not just another day. It's the last day I was married to Todd. And January 14 is going to be the last day I was married to Todd for the rest of my life. This whole year has been filled with 'a year ago this, a year ago that.' I'm sick of it. Anniversaries have a way of ripping open wounds I've spent months trying to close. This entire year has been filled with trying to forget the past. And I succeed pretty well until some anniversary comes along. It can be anything—his birthday, my birthday, the day we were married. Heck, I even go to pieces on the anniversary of the day we met! Can you believe it? And that was twelve years ago."

Yes, I could believe it. I could believe it because I've seen it happen so many times to so many people.

The Pain That Doesn't Go Away

Of all these anniversaries which arouse reminiscence, perhaps the most difficult to deal with is the date of a loved one's death. I recently had a student whose two-year-old son had died just months before she started back to college. When the baby had been born, the doctors had given him less than a year to live, but through "love, medicine, and miracles" he had grown into a toddler. Knowing this child would be with them only a short time, his parents had treasured each day he was theirs. On the first anniversary of his death, Dana, his mother, was in no shape to attend classes, but she came anyway. Later that day, she dropped by my office to talk. "For a year now I've carefully conditioned myself to accept a reality that I'd spent over two years preparing for, but today I find my emotions wearing thin. Over and over I keep reliving his life and his death. It's hard. It's really hard," she said. She was right. It is.

THE LOSSES OF THE PAST HOVER OVER OUR SHOULDERS

I, like Beth and Dana, know on an intellectual level that I must forget the pains of the past, but my emotions keep getting in the way of my mind. It's hard to practice what's so easy to say. I can sail along in complete control of my losses for weeks, even months, when something I see or hear will send me tumbling back in time.

I expect and am not surprised at the empty ache which accompanies anniversaries. Neither am I shocked when a photograph from the past pierces my soul. It hurts, but I'm not surprised. Still some pain sneaks up on me in the most unexpected moments. Time after time, some object will trigger tearing agony that I thought I'd gotten over. Wanting a neat and tidy end to loss, I convince myself that I'm emotionally prepared for these events which unexpectedly plunge me into the past. But I never am.

Recently I was doing the washing. As I reached into the tub of clean, damp clothes, mindlessly throwing garments over into the dryer, my hand opened on a white handkerchief with lovely butterflies in each corner, a handkerchief which used to be Mother's before her death and which is now mine. Sitting in the laundry, handkerchief in hand, I braced myself for the tears which came flowing down my face. Something so small, so seemingly insignificant, had brought back with haunting clarity the woman whose hands had held both the handkerchief and myself. Feeling like an abandoned orphan, I ached with loneliness as memories from the past overwhelmed me. I wish I could bring her back.

A few weeks later I was absent-mindedly watching an ad on television when suddenly a young woman was shown walking across the street in a fitted red wool coat. I felt the unexpected tears sliding down my face, and suddenly I was shaking with sobs, sobs for a nineteen-year-old girl named Barbara who used to walk across streets in a similar fitted red coat.

Loose Ends

We need to accept the fact that loss does not have a neat and tidy end. It is never over. And we need to realize it's normal, even necessary, to experience these recurring moments of pain.

Even though these intermittent lapses from living in the present are going to occur, we need not let them dominate our life. The strength that comes from living life a slice at a time allows these lapses into our life without destroying us.

An Awareness of the Now Diminishes Our Fear of the Future

Living in the present moment not only lessens these longings for yesterday; it also controls our fear of the future. The paradox of the human condition is that while we are content with the present, while we are on the very pinnacle of happiness, we are also in the valley of fear: fear that this wonderful contentment will not, cannot, last. Concentration on Now helps us deal with this paradox.

Focusing on What We Know

I've found that my fears can immobilize me if I don't keep a steady gaze on Now, today, this very hour. Since the wreck, I have never gone a day without pain in my legs. Although its intensity has varied from week to week, it has always been, and continues to be, my constant companion. A wise doctor once told me that the pain would always get worse when I was facing a situation I wasn't sure I could handle. And, without exception, it has. Because of this, I dread to start any new experience which has an uncertain outcome and, at times, am tempted to curl up in a safe little corner of the world and eliminate all change from my life. Any time I put my total attention on the outcome or results of what I'm attempting to do, any time I focus only on the future, I'm asking for trouble. But, ironically, I've found that I can work through—and lessen—the pain if I concentrate my energy and efforts on the present.

My life would be permanently immobile if I didn't consciously turn my attention away from the future and fasten it firmly on Now. Fear of illness, fear of old age, fear of death, fear of being dependent on someone, fear of being alone at the end of my life, fear of losing the use of my arms—a paraplegic has all the fears which haunt the human race, with some of them magnified because he's paralyzed. But by throwing my time and energy into today, I can make tomorrow's fears lessen and, for short periods, even disappear.

153

WHAT ACTIVITY MAKES YOU LOSE TRACK OF TIME? GIVE IT A HIGH PRIORITY IN YOUR LIFE

This living in the Now occurs each time we're doing something which totally absorbs us, something which keeps our full attention. Whenever we're enjoying a task so much that we lose track of time, we are fully present to the moment.

Many tasks and activities are like this. Recently when I asked numerous friends, "What activity do you enjoy doing so much that you lose track of time while doing it?," I got a variety of responses, but three or four kept repeating themselves. One woman said she enjoyed carpentry so much that when involved in a project, she easily could spend five hours and think it were two. Another said that when working in the garden, time became insignificant as she planted, weeded, and watered. Another's satisfaction came from reading. He said that he could easily lose all track of time whenever he was in the midst of a good book.

Can you remember the last time you were totally absorbed in a task, oblivious to everything but what you were enjoying at that moment? Chances are great that whatever you were doing should be given a larger chunk of your life than what you are now giving it. An activity we enjoy so much that it absorbs us to the point of losing track of time is probably something we should give a high priority. It can become a major tool as we work our way through loss and through life.

Some of us think this concept of living life one slice at a time is a good idea, but idealistic—not something a person can actually put into practice. We manufacture many reasons to avoid the present and wallow in our past pain and future fears. The one we use most is that it's just too hard to live in the Now.

Sure it's hard. If, however, we lived our life by avoiding the difficult and courting the easy, we'd be in a sorry mess. The difficulty of living life a slice at a time does not negate its effectiveness.

In this world, easy does not always equal effective. Many of the things which give life meaning are ideal in the sense we never reach them, we never master them: we simply keep striving toward them. "Ideals are like stars; you will not succeed in touching them with your hands. But like the seafaring man on the desert of waters, you choose them as your guides, and following them you will reach your destiny," said Carl Schurz in 1859. The truth of his words lives on in each of us who listens.

Ten Ways to Live in the "Now"

1. **Each morning as soon as you wake up, name the good things that are in your life at that moment. Be very specific.**

2. **Set miniature goals for yourself each morning** before getting out of bed. How do you want to act that day? What do you want to accomplish? Give yourself a positive set for the day ahead of you.

3. **Change your point of view from first person to second person, from "I" to "you."** Each time during the day when having a conversation with someone, try to look at those moments through his eyes. Try to make the day more pleasant for the person you're with at any given moment: the waitress, the clerk, the secretary, the janitor, the delivery boy.

4. **Slow down. Unclutter your calendar.** Make a conscious effort to slow your pace. If you find yourself pressured and hurrying, rushing to do something or get somewhere, ask yourself if you are cramming too many activities into one day. What are you rushing from or to, and why is the present unimportant?

5. **Find at least one positive aspect of every chore.** When in the midst of a job which has to be done, find some benefit that will come from doing that chore.

6. **Enjoy mealtime.** When eating—at home or in a restaurant—eat slowly, savor the food, enjoy the company, and talk of pleasant subjects.

7. **Set miniature goals for yourself before attending a social gathering.** Be specific. How do you

want to act? Name concrete behavior such as, "I'll find someone not actively engaged in the party and go talk with him" or "I'll compliment someone who looks especially nice."

8. **Monitor your mind.** Listen to the verbal messages you send yourself. When you hear yourself fearing future old age, illness, financial failure, or death, intently focus your attention on what you will be doing in the next five minutes.

9. **Each evening make a mental list of the good things that entered your life that day.** Be specific. Name people, places, and events that made the day meaningful and satisfying.

10. **Make a list of activities you enjoy so much that they make you lose track of time.** Make these a high priority in your life and give them large amounts of your time and energy.

Moving On

Our awareness of the present moment enables all of us who have experienced loss to see that yesterday is gone and tomorrow does not exist.

Attempting to give me hope following the wreck in 1955, a doctor assured me that "paraplegics live about twenty years." Unfortunately I took him very seriously. The words which were meant to motivate me back into the mainstream were to ripple through the next twenty years of my life and hideously haunt me as I approached 1975.

Although twenty years seemed like an eternity when I was nineteen, weeks quickly became months and turned into years. Suddenly I was thirty-nine. Even though the doctor's words had been true when he said them, by 1975 the miracles of science had made the figure obsolete. My mind knew it was obsolete, but my emotions did a beautiful job of ignoring my mind. And these emotions filled me with fear for my future.

As I passed that twenty-year milestone and moved on, I realized how transitory life is. That realization has changed my life. After now being a paraplegic for over thirty years, I'm living well past my normal life expectancy. And I'm always aware that I'm living on "borrowed time."

But each of us is living on borrowed time; each of us is trembling tenaciously on the edge of eternity. By choosing to ignore the fact that we're terminal, we fail to live in the Now. But a realization of life's brevity brings an appreciation of its beauty. This brevity and beauty add a new dimension to the present moment.

By cutting life up into small slices and living one slice at a time, we discover that indeed the best time is Now.

INVESTING IN SOLITUDE

"By all means use sometimes to be alone. Salute thyself; see what thy soul does wear . . . Who cannot rest till he good fellows find, He breaks up house, turns out of doors his mind."
George Herbert, "The Church-Porch," Stanza 25

Although the strength to face loss is within each of us, it often lies latent. We don't come into this world with fully developed internal resources. Rather, they are carefully cultivated during all of the quiet moments we spend alone, by ourselves and with ourselves.

This cultivation requires an investment in solitude, an investment some of us find difficult to make, even though making it would yield the dividends we so desire.

Some of our richest moments can be those we spend alone, moments in which we re-create ourselves and discover all the layers of life within us. During these times when we do absolutely nothing but get acquainted with our inner self, we are taking what Dag Hammarskjold calls "the longest journey," the journey inward. These quiet times help us to put life's parts in perspective. Through them we cultivate our internal resources and gain the strength needed to sustain us in the chaos of loss.

For many of us, however, the fear of being alone is so great that we refuse to risk this investment in solitude.

THE PANIC OF BEING ALONE

While reading the essay "Channeled Whelk" by Anne Morrow Lindbergh, my students talk about this fear. In the essay, Lindbergh goes by herself to a quiet cabin, shedding as many modern conveniences as possible, and finds there new inner strength, strength she will use when she goes back to face the obligations and distractions of life. It's a thought-provoking essay and lends itself to good classroom discussion about the value of being alone.

Invariably, when asked, "Would you want to spend a week alone without TV, radio, or stereo?" my students send back a chorus of "No's." The sad part is that those "No's" are tinged with fear. "I can't stand to be alone" is the lament of the present generation. These teens are passionately frightened at the prospect of having only themselves for company. Sensing the anxiety my question has aroused, I query, "Why not?" Always I get the same reply, "What would I do?"

We have created a generation that is afraid to be alone. Never having had only themselves for companions, they are overwhelmed at the prospect of spending one day, let alone one week, in an empty house or a quiet park. Alone. No headphones, no TV, no radio, no compact disc player, no stereo. During their entire lives, something, or someone, has always entertained them. Totally dependent on outer stimuli, they have become passive observers of life. Having no internal resources to draw on, they fear solitude.

This fear has filtered down from the generation which raised them. Listen to what their parents are saying. "I have to get a job now that the children are grown. I'll go crazy staying by myself all day," says a friend. A colleague announces, "I go batty when I'm in the house alone." An adult student comments, "There are times I go shopping just to avoid being alone." Another confides, "I came back to college because I can't stand staying at home and doing nothing."

Although we may fear being alone, loss often gives us no choice. Since most significant losses are followed by a period of aloneness, it might be hypothesized that loss automatically brings inner growth. Reality tells us differently. Being alone is no guarantee that we will become a stronger person.

Being *BY* Ourselves Does Not Assure Being *WITH* Ourselves

All of us are by ourselves once in a while. Although we may try to avoid these situations, now and then we discover that the house is empty and we're alone.

When *with* ourselves, we'll be listening to our thoughts and feelings, involved in an inner dialogue, an endless stream of commentary concerning ourselves and our world. We'll have conversations with the person inside us and discover he gives us new insights concerning the business of living. We'll soon feel as comfortable with our inner self as we would with another person. We'll find that we agree with Thoreau when he says, "I love to be alone. I never found a companion that was so companionable as solitude."

We'll do this, however, only if we're aware of the difference between being *by* one's self and being *with* one's self. It's easy to be alone, to be by ourselves, and totally avoid having any kind of an inner dialogue. Only scratching the surface of our self-awareness, seldom probing the inner recesses of our minds and souls, we manage to keep our thoughts masked, fearing to face what we'll find underneath.

Because loss brings periods of aloneness, it can be the catalyst for tearing off this mask and listening to ourselves. Once we realize that the seeds for inner awareness are sown in solitude, we welcome time to be alone, time to retreat from the world.

But we soon discover how difficult it is in our society to find either the time or the place for retreat and aloneness. We over-schedule our lives and then decide we have no time left for solitude or silence. We refuse to turn off our TV's, stereos, and radios, and then tell ourselves that we have no quiet place for thought or reflection. We have neither the time nor the place because we choose to have neither.

BUSYNESS IS ONE WAY WE AVOID SELF-AWARENESS

One way we choose to effectively block any opportunity for inner dialogue is by staying perpetually busy. This busyness becomes our way of keeping self-awareness at bay.

We clutter our calendar and our life with "things to do." "I'm so busy," we say. "I've got appointments, conferences, committee meetings every day this week." And then we add, "My calendar is so full that I don't have a free moment for myself." And we say it with just a hint of pride, implying that our busyness is a reflection of our importance, our value as a person.

Indeed, society does lead us to see our worth in relation to the speed with which we rush through life, the number of activities we can cram into a day. Because of this preoccupation with numbers, "What did you do today?" causes us to enumerate all the tasks we attempted or completed in the last twenty-four-hour period. The question carries with it the implicit assumption that more is better.

If I reply, "I graded fifteen essay tests, hemmed that brown skirt, made bread, and washed the clothes," society says, "You've been a productive person. You've accomplished a lot." But if I reply, "I spent the day on the deck reading and thinking," society translates this into "You goofed off and did nothing." Yet, I may have accomplished more when I read and thought than when I graded, sewed, baked, and washed.

In Our Society, More Is Better

One of the most popular avenues used for keeping busy is the sixty-hour work week, a phenomenon society not only approves, but applauds. People say that work is good, without considering what motivates the working person and without distinguishing between moderate and excessive. Who faults the agent who spends his evenings writing reports, contacting clients, or creating new sales strategies? Who criticizes the professor who asks for overloads, teaches summer school, and spends ten hours on campus each day? No one. In fact, people will praise him, calling him a good worker and a good provider, when he may, in reality, be a person who wants nothing to do with his inner self.

Because our society worships this assumption that more is better, it encourages us to juggle two things at once. A student studies lessons while listening to the stereo, a family eats dinner while watching television, and a businessman drives his car while dictating a letter. And we've all caught ourselves talking on the phone while balancing a checkbook, paying bills, or writing notes.

Marketing executives have gotten a whiff of this mania for juggling life and are using it to their advantage. Many supermarkets recently put in salad bars and encouraged people to "make your salad and take it with you." Presto! Eating and shopping were added to the list of things a person could do simultaneously. Within a week of hearing the ad, I saw a woman pushing a grocery cart, eating a tossed salad, and reaching for items on her shopping list. Our society had found an additional way to stuff another activity into an already overloaded day.

Yet, even as we fill our lives with this network of tasks and appointments, piling one on top of another, a little corner of us is usually aware that many of our commitments are neither wanted nor needed. We find ourselves tripping through a life of trivial busy-ness—committee meetings which are meaningless, social engagements which are superficial, hobbies which have become habits. Being busy becomes a way of life. Too often we find ourselves getting involved in activities more by default than by design.

We're Killing More than Time

We say we're "killing time," but actually we're killing much more than just time. Since each person's life consists of a limited number of hours each day, we don't kill time; we kill life. People all around us are committing suicide daily.

Still, even knowing this, we cling to our calendars as if they were our support systems. In time, we find the appointments, engagements, meetings, and tasks have taken on an identity in and of themselves. We discover they control us. We're now at the mercy of our date books.

Because we live in a society which doesn't want to say "No" to anything, we pack into our few waking hours every possible experience that attracts us. No matter that it's impossible to enjoy everything we're doing. Rather than say "No" to an activity, we dabble in them all, stretching our lives so thin that the slightest pressure punctures our inner calm. Rather than sim-plify our lives and fully feast on each portion, we settle for nibbling on everything we can reach in the smorgasbord of life, tasting all, but enjoying none.

Recognizing that we have chosen to mire ourselves in this mud of busyness, only we can pull ourselves out of it.

What Ever Happened to the Fine Art of Doing Nothing?

What has created this mania for keeping busy? Why can't people sit still without guilt? Why is "doing nothing" the sin of the twentieth century?

In a number-oriented society such as ours, people want growth to be measurable. Internal growth is not. Therefore, any time we allow ourselves the "luxury" of doing nothing, we'll feel guilty. Because we live in a society where it's a virtue to be busy, but a vice to do nothing, each time we pause for reflection, we'll be swimming upstream against that value system. Having had it pounded into us for so long that busyness is good, we'll find it difficult to shake loose of that philosophy. A significant loss, however, often shakes us loose. We find that while causing our lives to race headlong through a series of circles, this busyness hinders our healing.

As a result of our fear of being alone, of knowing our inner self, we've lost the fine art of doing nothing. In its passing has gone one of our most valuable internal resources.

BY FILLING OUR LIVES WITH NOISE, WE AVOID SELF-AWARENESS

Another well-used way of refusing to get in touch with ourselves is by filling our lives with noise. In our society today, silence is an enemy to be conquered. People will go to great lengths and expense—both financially and spiritually—to obliterate any moments of silence that might inadvertently creep into the crevices of their world.

What's the Noise Level of Your Life?

Fill in the blank with a 3, 2, or 1, using the following scale:

Often   (3)   Sometimes   (2)   Rarely   (1)

____ 1. I turn on the car radio or the cassette player as soon as I start the engine.

____ 2. Getting home after work, I turn on the TV or radio as soon as I enter the house.

____ 3. I watch TV while eating the evening meal.

____ 4. I wear headphones while jogging, bicycling, running, or walking.

____ 5. I take the portable TV with me when I am picnicking, camping, or fishing.

____ 6. I feel uncomfortable when the family is away and the house is silent.

____ 7. I'd rather watch television or a video than sit in silence sewing, reading, knitting, painting, writing, or working crossword puzzles.

____ 8. While preparing meals, I listen to the radio, TV, or stereo.

____ 9. I dislike spending vacations at places where I have no access to TV or radio.

____ 10. I feel guilty if I spend an hour quietly sitting, thinking, and doing "absolutely nothing."

If your score is over 15, you may need to lower the noise level in your life.

Turn It Down!

Each room in our modern home comes equipped with numerous devices to assure us that we will never have to deal with silence. Radios, televisions, compact disc players, and cassette recorders continually clamor for our attention—and usually get it. In the bedroom we have a radio which wakes us to music, weather, and commercials, repeats the process as we finish our day, and conveniently turns itself off after we have gone to sleep. In the kitchen we

discover the automated miracles which have simpli-
fied our lives have taken away our peace and quiet,
even as they've given us wonderful conveniences.
The sounds of the automatic dishwasher, garbage
disposal, ice-cube maker, microwave oven, food
processor, mixmaster, blender, and electric can
opener all compete with the omnipresent radio or
television, making conversation with others, let alone
with one's self, nearly impossible.

Even our car is now equipped to eliminate silence. The
radio is turned on immediately after the motor is
started, never to be turned off until the engine is.
Many people, believing that the radio is not a suffi-
cient deterrent against quiet, add tape decks or compact disc players—all, of course, with stereo speakers.
Recently telephones and televisions have been added
as insurance that we will never have to contend with
silence.

In fact, society has recently brought a new dimension
to the flight from solitude. As the ultimate escape—
from silence and from themselves—they have guaran-
teed never-ending noise by wearing headphones while
walking, jogging, bicycling, or driving. It doesn't matter where the person is or what he's doing: the headphones go on.

Another twentieth century source of noise is the television. This noise (be it from miniature, portable, con-
sole, or big screen) has become a quick, easy, and

socially acceptable way to escape self-awareness. Rather than actively participate in our own thoughts, we prefer to absorb someone else's. While lying in the backyard getting a suntan, fishing at a lake in the wilderness, or camping at a national park, people now carry with them their portable TVs, which not only keep them from experiencing silence, but do a rather good job of assuring no one near them experiences it either.

Until we've experienced the value of solitude, we'll continue using noise and busyness as a shield against self-awareness. We're actually hiding behind a wall of sound!

Noise and Busyness Impoverish Us

Often, it takes the jolt of a significant loss to make us aware that our reliance on this shield has impoverished us. Reaching inside ourselves for inner strength, we find an empty room. And suddenly, for perhaps the first time in our lives, we realize the value of internal resources and the solitude in which they are developed. So how are we going to get this needed aloneness, this silence, this solitude back into our life?

One solution would be a total retreat. We all have those moments when we'd like to withdraw with the monks, away from the noise and distractions of our immediate surroundings. Although retreat may tempt us at times, it usually is not the answer. Regardless of how much we may wish to momentarily leave the rush of life, we're aware that being in it assures us that we are a part of others' joys and fears and they are part of ours. Although total retreat may be a workable and satisfactory solution for some, it isn't realistic nor even desirable for most of us.

We need not, however, make a commitment to total silence in order to know the benefits of solitude. We need only make a commitment of bits and pieces of our time each week. A half-hour here, an hour there— slowly we find the times and the places to be alone. We need to plan these moments into our life. Solitude won't magically occur; we must create it.

Ten Ways to Cultivate Solitude

1. **Be selective about what you watch on TV.** Limit your viewing to only a few special shows each week.

2. **Drive with your radio and cassette player turned off.** After doing this for a few days, you will find yourself having interesting internal dialogues.

3. **Unclutter your calendar.** Rid your life of pressure from appointments by saying "No" to

meaningless meetings and superficial social engagements.

4. **Plan "retreat" time into each day.** Go into your bedroom or study, close the door, and announce that you are not to be disturbed. Allow yourself time to recharge, even if it's only fifteen minutes a day.

5. **Go places and do things alone now and then.** Each of us needs time alone. Rake leaves, pull weeds, go to the park, sit on the deck—alone.

6. **End the day in a relaxed atmosphere.** Read a book or listen to tranquil music.

7. **Avoid listening to or watching the news right before going to sleep.** Also as your last activity of the day, avoid watching TV programs or videos filled with violence.

8. **While doing daily tasks, turn off the radio, stereo, and TV.** While washing the dishes, balancing a checkbook, or taking a bath, give yourself the gift of solitude.

9. **While working in the yard, take off the Walkman.** Mowing the lawn, walking the dog, or trimming the shrubs are good opportunities for thought.

10. **When sunbathing, fishing, or camping, leave your portable TV and your Walkman at home.** Listen to your own thoughts rather than someone else's.

GETTING TO KNOW OURSELVES

By constantly recharging our internal batteries and rejuvenating ourselves, we can create an inner stability and serenity that will strengthen not only us, but every life we touch. We can't give something away we don't first have ourselves, so when our pitcher gets empty, we need to refill it.

The question becomes, "What activities and settings will promote my inner growth? How can I refresh and re-create myself?"

One way is to occasionally allow ourselves the luxury of doing absolutely nothing. Practicing for a while, we'll learn not only to tolerate, but actually to crave, this aloneness. We'll find when we allow ourselves to sit quietly alone, doing nothing but thinking, our mind goes in interesting spirals, uncovering feelings and ideas we've been hiding even from ourselves.

Doing nothing, however, is only one way to use solitude. When done alone and in silence, many daily activities can refresh and re-create. While doing such tasks, a person gives her mind the opportunity to wander and refresh itself. Some find gardening, bicycling, and painting to be such activities, but there are no "right" activities which should be done to cultivate our internal resources. The activities I choose—observing nature, reading books, writing

174

ideas, talking to God—give me a renewal, a starting over, a fresh perspective. All require silence and solitude for this renewal to take place.

OBSERVING NATURE CULTIVATES OUR INTERNAL RESOURCES

We're not born with an appreciation of nature. Neither is it taught. It's caught. It's caught from those around us who already have it. Some people have parents who make this catching very easy. I'm one of these fortunate few.

One spring evening when I was in college hurriedly stirring gravy and trying to quickly get supper on the table, my father called from the living room, "Come here and look at this beautiful sunset." "Not now, I can't leave the gravy; it'll get lumpy," I replied. From the other room came my mother's response: "Set it off the burner and come look. We can make gravy any night, but a sunset like this just comes now and then." Because my life was peppered with incidents such as this, observing nature became an important part of my life.

Nature's Reassuring Patterns

I've found nature to be a mirror, teaching us a great deal about ourselves and the world in which we live.

Its enduring pattern of predictability brings a calm reassurance into our lives.

This predictability is seen clearly in the changing seasons. It's reassuring to know that each April, regardless of what is going on in our own lives, the world around us will turn yellow, as daffodils, forsythia, and goldfinch all remind us that spring has arrived. With a sense of security, we then look forward to the hot sun shining through the leaves, making summer shadows that are possible only during that time of the year. We know that every autumn the oaks will turn red, the maples gold, with the variegated gums becoming first a translucent yellow, later a rich amber. We can predict with certainty that the leaves will drop first from the tulip trees, followed by the river birches, ashes, and maples, with the oaks and beeches holding foliage far into December. We know that each winter, without fail, we can count on the cardinals, bluejays, and red-bellied woodpeckers to sprinkle splashes of red and blue color on the crusty snow during the daytime, while the moon makes shadowed rings on the white carpet at night. Then before we know it, the world turns yellow and we start the predictable cycle again.

The normal cyclic patterns of nature, barring catastrophe or devastation, bring a calming reassurance. All of us fear death, yet nature shows us that death is a part of the cycle of life. All around us we watch birds, squirrels, rabbits, and chipmunks living with an unknowing acceptance of these cycles, without fear or concern. Observing this can have a peaceful, calming effect as we see our niches in a larger pattern. In it we are reminded of the rhythms of life, the ebb and flow of which we ourselves are so much a part.

Nature's Individuality

The individuality which exists within these predictable patterns shows us in yet another way that nature mirrors life. I see this individuality clearly in the birds which visit. Each has its own unique personality. The black-capped chickadee won't sit still for a second, grabbing seeds from the suet cake and flying to the safety of a tree; but the downy woodpecker will cling tenaciously, eating for five minutes at a time, oblivious to the other birds waiting their turn. Whereas the red-bellied woodpecker madly sweeps the sunflower seed on the ground, searching for exactly the one he wants, the yellow-shafted flicker eats whatever seed happens to be near the front of the feeder, content with what is readily available. And the bold bluejay sits only three feet away from me on the deck railing, talking loudly to the birds beside him, asserting his right of domain even while sharing it, but the skittish tufted titmouse watches me from a distance, carefully keeping himself half-hidden in the privacy of a tree. These differences mirror the individuality which exists in people and remind me of the uniqueness in each of us.

A Growing Awareness

Observing nature brings awareness of the continuity and recovery that goes on all the time at every layer of life. Seeing a tiny twig grow into a towering poplar, noticing the tips of the English ivy get light green each spring, observing the ash tree become symmetrical again after having had branches chopped from it, or watching a new batch of juvenile birds furiously flutter their wings, waiting for their parents to feed them—all remind me of the continuity and enduring cycles of nature.

Perhaps one of the best analogies of recovery is in the bird who accidentally flies into our glass sliding door, unaware that we have invaded its territory. It will lie very still—sometimes for over an hour—waiting for its body to get over the shock. Watching and waiting to see if the injured bird will make it up again, I think what a lesson we humans could learn if we would. When we're stunned by life, when we run into the unexpected and are knocked down, we also need to sit still while we regain the strength to resume our regular pattern of living.

Threaded throughout my year—from the blinking lightning bugs of summer, the kaleidoscope of red, rust, and yellow in autumn, the silent, velvet hush of winter snow, to the fragile beauty of purple crocus in the spring—is a peace and contentment that money cannot buy. Even on days when my professional or personal life is chaos, I regain stability from smelling the night air as the moon rises over the woods, seeing the goldfinch make yellow rollercoaster trips from tree to tree, and watching the hummingbirds. Sara Teasdale tells us in the poem "Barter" that "Life has loveliness to sell." I've found that I'm a richer person when I take the time to accept the gift it offers.

Eight Ways to Cultivate an Appreciation of Nature

1. **Choose to walk, rather than drive.** When you have a choice between driving or walking, walk. Notice what is going on around you. What birds do you see? What flowers, shrubs, or trees? Enjoy the feel of the warm sun, the wet rain, the cool breeze, or the crisp cold.

2. **Stay alert to the changing panorama of the trees.** Be aware which trees bud first in the spring and which drop leaves first in the fall. While raking, notice which trees shed yellow, red, or russet color leaves and how the shapes of the leaves differ.

3. **Learn to recognize shrubs and flowers in your neighborhood.** Many community colleges, high schools, and nature preserves offer non-credit

courses for just this purpose. With increased knowledge comes increased awareness.

4. **Invest in a bird feeder and one of Peterson's bird books.** After placing the feeder near a window where you often stand or sit, take fifteen minutes each day and watch what birds come into your life. Keep a diary of which ones visit you.

5. **Keep a pair of binoculars on a table near the window.** Having them readily available will increase their use significantly.

6. **Make watching nature a part of your daily routine.** To ensure a sense of routine, associate it with some daily task such as eating breakfast or folding clean clothes. Do the task you've chosen near the window, staying alert to everything that is going on outside.

7. **Take some of your vacations away from any city.** There are many retreat areas in our country such as state parks, national parks, nature preserves, wilderness areas, and local wildlife districts. Take advantage of these.

8. **Show your children the beauty of nature.** Make a habit of sprinkling each day with, "Look at the sunset" "Watch the rollercoaster flight of those goldfinch" and "See that beautiful full moon." Fill your children's lives with the "Look," "Watch," and "See" of nature's beauty.

READING BOOKS CULTIVATES OUR INTERNAL RESOURCES

As I search for activities to strengthen my internal resources, I find myself repeatedly turning to books. The more I reach out to others, the more I need the ideas and insights which I get from them.

Magazines and Newspapers Are Transient, but Books Are Permanent

I used to read everything I could get my hands on; newspapers, magazines, and books filled my free hours. But as I became aware that saying "Yes" to some things meant saying "No" to others, I found myself turning more often to books and less to newspapers and magazines. I quit trying to read the six magazines which came to my home each month and settled for subscribing to three; I quit taking the daily paper and had only the Sunday edition delivered. In the hours I had previously spent on these magazines and newspapers, I now read more books.

Because we live in a time-oriented society, we have grown accustomed to skimming through life. We want things fast, and we want them short—whether it's food for our bodies or food for our minds. So we flip through magazines, reading here and there, remembering next-to-nothing of what we've read.

While magazines are transient, books are permanent; while magazines are gulped, books are sipped; while magazines quickly enter the trash can, books linger on the shelves of our homes—and the shelves of our mind. Books give us a stability that is impossible to find in newspapers or magazines. It would be impossible to name one magazine that has changed my life, yet many books have.

In our society with its throw-away mentality, books give us a permanence that is needed. I've found there is a correlation between the significance of ideas and the length of time since they've been printed. Much that is printed in newspapers and magazines is trivial, insignificant, and dated within a few weeks. I now see why Emerson says, "Never read any book that is not a year old."

Books
Shape Personality

Reading is a good way to "refill my pitcher," because what I put in splashes out onto others. Within days of reading an idea, I've often found I needed it when talking to a student. Repeatedly I have been able to pull out of my mind an idea I've recently read—an idea that was not there previously. Had I not read it, I would not have had it in my mind and could not have shared it. I often wonder if I'm not guided to read things so I'll have them to share later.

I have hungrily read everything written by John Powell and Eugene Kennedy and have shared their minds with many. Their books seem to have been written just for me. Indeed, perhaps they were. Why do we pick up one book in a bookstore and ignore the one beside it? Writers have pondered that for decades. I spend hours sitting in our local bookstore (luckily I bring my own chair) reading blurbs, backs, and first chapters of books. Always open to suggestions from fellow customers, I carefully choose the books I want to buy. One day years ago as I was close to purchasing John Powells' *Unconditional Love,* a kind gentleman standing near me said, "Buy it. You'll never be sorry." I did, and I haven't been.

I stumbled on Eugene Kennedy's mind in much the same way. Knowing that following surgery I would be spending two months in bed on my stomach, I was in the bookstore buying books. Picking up *The Pain of Being Human,* I complained about the tiny print and the "stupid" cover. As I was doing so, the cliche "Never judge a book by its cover" flashed through my mind. Somewhat as an act of contrition for my superficial judgement, I purchased the book, only to find after reading it that I'd brushed my mind against the mind of a man who was to change not only my life but the lives of many troubled students. I met a man whose love for God and the human race was matched by his obvious love affair with the English language. His innovative and beautiful similies and metaphors gave depth to everything he said.

WRITING CULTIVATES OUR INTERNAL RESOURCES

I've found that writing is another road that leads to self-awareness. Whenever I sit down and write for an hour, I end up knowing more about myself than I did sixty minutes earlier. This is true whether I'm writing to a friend or to myself.

Writing became a large part of my life as a response to the barrier created by the wheelchair. I found the chair enclosed me in a shell, making it difficult to reach people easily. Always, always, the barrier was there. I couldn't get to people across a crowded room, in the next house, or in another town. Communication became impossible. An important part of my life was missing. Writing allows me movement while it opens my heart and mind.

The Inadequacy of Five-Minute Phone Calls

If we don't communicate, we are like individual islands, and we never touch. I sit here with my feelings all locked up inside me, and you sit over there wondering what I'm feeling while you too are locked in your own little world. Communication is what keeps us human, and yet our society has hurried its pace and set its priorities so that sharing of thoughts and feelings has been pushed aside.

When we reach out and touch someone, it's more often with a five-minute phone call than a five-page letter.

Yet, who wouldn't rather get the letter? Who doesn't flip through the numerous ads, bills, and junk mail hoping for just one real letter? Who doesn't ask of the person carrying the mail into the house, "Is there anything important?"—meaning is there a letter in that mass of generic envelopes marked **CAR-RT SORT**. We crave letters because they are gifts. We sense that someone has given up some of his time, some of his energy, and rearranged his schedule to include us. Someone has decided we're more important than washing the windows or watching television.

Realizing that I could no longer hop in the car or run across the street to talk to friends, I started using letters as an alternative form of communication. And in the process of giving someone else a gift, I gave myself one. While writing copiously and constantly, I found an avenue for self-understanding. In order to put all the daily frustrations, fears, and joys into my letter, I had to organize my thoughts. As I shared with others what I'd been thinking and doing, those thoughts and actions became clearer to me.

A Typewriter Can Be a Psychiatrist

When I reached a point where my life was shattering

all around me, I began writing not to friends, but to myself.

Needing to ventilate the mental stress whirling through me, I talked daily to my paper psychiatrist, a thirty-year-old, manual Remington Rand typewriter. Each day after work I'd type for an hour or more, telling my typewriter all the feelings I was experiencing, taking care to vent every emotion that was inside me. Because I knew no one but me would read what I was writing, I poured out things I could not have told anyone else. Even after this rough point in my life smoothed out, I continued to type. I did this daily for over five years. I learned from the experience that writing is an effective way to give life focus, that putting my thoughts and feelings on paper forces me to clarify issues. I found that the very act of forming words and making sentences out of my life helps me understand it.

I live a richer, more meaningful life because it is one filled with written words. Reading and writing are more to me than a hobby or a profession. Reading and writing *are* me. I am what I have read, and I become what I write. Words help me form my ideas, clarify my values, and shape my destiny. Without question, they strengthen my internal resources. They are also a record and a yardstick of my life's journey. They enable me to see where I've been, how far I've come, and how much I've grown.

TALKING TO GOD CULTIVATES OUR INTERNAL RESOURCES

Woven throughout the tapestry of my life and forming the essential thread in it is God. All other strands are interlaced with this one central source of meaning.

Although one of my parents was raised in the Methodist church and the other in the Catholic, my beliefs don't fit neatly into either. They do, however, fit into both. The God I talk to daily, often hourly, is the center core of my life. He is more a verb than a noun, the Love that gives me the courage and strength to walk through loss.

When loss walks in and crumbles our world, we suddenly realize it's going to be just God and us against the pain. The rejection, the emptiness, the loss—all make us vividly aware of our need for a close communication with this God we're walking through loss with now and will be walking through life with later.

It doesn't take long to realize we feel God's presence most clearly in the absence of distractions. While going through loss, the verse "Be still and know that I am God" strikes a receptive chord. We realize that only by "being still" can we cultivate and nourish our relationship with God. Realizing this, we crave more solitude, more time alone. It isn't that God is any less present amidst the clamor and noise of life; it's simply that we aren't aware of our need for Him.

A Need for a Quiet Place

Noise and busyness, the twentieth century opiates, deaden our minds and our souls. They keep us preoccupied and busy with trivial things that are totally unimportant when loss enters our life. As we shuffle our priorities, we seek solitude.

Taking the risk of aloneness helps us develop the strength to meet life with all its inherent losses, present and future. This strength is available to each of us who takes the time to listen. Our inner voice talks to us all the time, but unless we unclutter our lives, we never hear what it's saying. As we strip away the noise and busyness, we discover our internal resources.

Only with deliberate planning, however, will this stripping get done. We, and we alone, develop this potential that is within us. We choose to develop it when we welcome bits and pieces of solitude into our life.

KNOWING THIS
TOO WILL PASS

> *"The greatest mortal*
> *consolation, which we derive*
> *from the transitoriness of all*
> *things—from the right of*
> *saying, in every conjuncture,*
> *'This, too, will pass away.'"*
> Nathaniel Hawthorne,
> *The Marble Faun.* 16

On an October afternoon a few years ago, Sara, a good-looking, eighteen-year-old girl I'd had in first-year English, was sitting crosslegged on the carpet of my living room. She had called a few hours earlier asking if she could come over and "talk about life." Yet, as we talked, we both knew our conversation was not just about life. Sara was trying to find meaning in a world that had hurt her. "Why live?" she asked. Since she had already attempted suicide once before, I knew her question wasn't entirely hypothetical.

The autumn sun streamed across her auburn hair as she continued, "I just don't see how you can say that life is worth living after all you've gone through." So I talked of reasons why life might be worth living, why people might decide to deal with a less-than-perfect world. As I talked she took notes, much as if she were still my pupil. After listing all the pros and cons we could think of concerning killing one's self, we agreed that suicide, seductive as it might seem at times, wasn't the answer.

As dusk filled the living room, we continued to discuss her ambivalence. "How can you be so objective? Have you ever thought that life wasn't worth the effort? Didn't you ever want to quit living?" she asked.

"Oh, yes," I replied.

"But you didn't," she answered. "Why didn't you?"

Trying to answer her with perfect honesty, I said, "The first time I wanted to kill myself, I thought it was a sin to do so. I'm sure that belief prevented me. But as I got older, I had other times when dying seemed preferable to living. And by then I had something else stopping me. Experience. There's a vast difference between being eighteen and being forty-eight."

I looked at her youthful beauty and said, "You're eighteen. You've never come through a devastating loss, and you're sure there will be no coming through this one. Your emotional pain at this moment is so great that suicide seems a sensible, even appealing, solution. You're sure this is the end of life. With age, you'll realize each loss is not the end of life, but a part of life. You'll realize this because you will have been there before and you will have come through."

I continued, "I've been there. Over and over and over I've hit rock bottom. Over and over and over I've felt helpless, unloved, unneeded. But because I've been there and come through it, I know I can do it. It's not fair, but age gives me an advantage over you in that department."

"You see, Sara," I explained, "Although the loss itself never leaves us, we become aware that life goes on. Most grief is finite. Although the loss may be permanent, the grief isn't. But when in the midst of loss, a person has a lack of perspective. And if that person is a teenager, his perspective is even more distorted. His pain is overwhelming and the future holds no promises but continued pain. His youth alone makes it impossible for him to see that the current pain is limited."

I told her that because I was older than she, I knew something she'd learn later in life and that was "This too shall pass." I'd learned that only after suffering numerous losses—large and small—do we finally see ourselves repeatedly working our way through each one, coming out on the other side, ready to go on with life.

From cradle to grave we do a great deal of growing and changing. Some of these changes are pleasant and enjoyable, while others are painful and difficult. To live is to change. And one of these changes that will always be a part of our lives is loss. As we move from one phase of life to the next, we're always going to leave something behind. Since we're always growing, always becoming, we are also always changing. But loss is an implicit part of change.

Losing Is a Vital Part of Living

So the question is never, "Will there be another loss in my life?" There will. Loss is repetitious. As we work our way through life, we begin to see that loss never ends. Slowly we begin to realize that it is an inherent part of being alive and will reoccur as long as we are breathing. And slowly we accept that fact. Then just when we begin to feel whole again, another loss will rip through our lives, leaving us picking up the fragments of our newly shattered soul.

Although we want a neat and tidy end to our loss, none exists. Although we want our problems solved and finished, the problem of loss can't be solved—and it's never finished. There will never be a day when we will say, "It's over. I'm whole now. I'm healed and ready to get on with my life." Although there may be moments when we will feel we're partially glued together, there will be others when we're sure we're not. Healing is never finished. As we live each day, we'll find fresh cracks and breaks in our lives, and we won't always handle them well. We'll find there are some days when putting ourselves back together demands more energy than we possess.

People are forever asking me, "How do you keep your morale up all the time? How do you stay so positive every day?" The answer is, "I don't." I have low days; everyone has low days. I accept those days as a part of being human. All I can do is know they're going to happen and be prepared for the inevitable. Everyone is less than perfect, but each of us believes that he should be the exception. When we find our soul is blemished, we grimace and feel inadequate. But we must allow ourselves these imperfections. There are days I find it nearly impossible to accept the losses that have entered my life. Accepting loss is hard work. One cultivates attitudes, makes choices, and shifts values so he can finally heal.

And the sooner the better. Knowing that loss will always be a part of life helps us ready ourselves for the inevitable. We realize that once we finally heal from one loss, another is heading down the road toward us. The best time to prepare for it is before it occurs. By cultivating our internal resources, we can do just that. We will then find within us the strength to meet life with all its inherent losses, present and future.